Historical Reflections

MAUGHON AND NORTON FAMILY OF PIKE COUNTY ALABAMA

DEBORAH LYNN SUTTON

outskirts press

Historical Reflections of the Maughon and Norton Family of Pike County Alabama
All Rights Reserved.
Copyright © 2020 Deborah Lynn Sutton
v2.0

The opinions expressed in this manuscript are solely the opinions of the author and do not represent the opinions or thoughts of the publisher. The author has represented and warranted full ownership and/or legal right to publish all the materials in this book.

This book may not be reproduced, transmitted, or stored in whole or in part by any means, including graphic, electronic, or mechanical without the express written consent of the publisher except in the case of brief quotations embodied in critical articles and reviews.

Outskirts Press, Inc.
http://www.outskirtspress.com

ISBN: 978-1-9772-2750-8

Cover Photo © 2020 www.gettyimages.com. All rights reserved - used with permission.

Outskirts Press and the "OP" logo are trademarks belonging to Outskirts Press, Inc.

PRINTED IN THE UNITED STATES OF AMERICA

Table of Contents

Preface i

Part One: The Maughon Family: From Their Beginning 1

Part Two: From Walton County, Georgia To Pike County, Alabama 7

Source Information 124

Preface

THIS WORK REFLECTS the love and respect for my ancestors and the life and times that they lived. Their struggles were real and they knew the value of life and what life has to offer. The families mentioned in this book set amazing examples of humanity and are perfect examples of real life. The information contained herein has been derived from eight years of research on records obtained from the National Archives as well as from handed down family history. My mission was to be able to share the family ancestry for years to come and to preserve the memory of my family to all of those whom are yet to come. If anyone or anything has been overlooked or left out, I sincerely apologize, for it wasn't intentional. This work is dedicated to my grandfather, Frazier Norton and his sweet mother, (Maw) Lonnie Ophelia Maughon Norton. They would be extremely proud of their ancestors for keeping the memories vibrant of the family that they were so proud to claim. It is from whence these ancestors were passed along to me and mine. It is from whence they will forever be remembered.

Deborah Lynn Berry Sutton

Part One

The Maughon Family: From Their Beginning

THE MAUGHON FAMILY roots are of Irish-Scottish descent. Born in Ireland in 1727, William Maughon, Sr. (1727-1795) immigrated to the United States as a young man sometime during the 1740's to find fame and fortune and a new life for himself and his family. He was certain that better things awaited him across the mighty waters in the United States. Upon arriving in North Hampton, North Carolina he soon became acquainted with a young lady by the name of Nancy. They were soon married and by 1750 their first son, William Maughon, Jr. was born. William Maughon, Jr. would be the first among this line of the Maughon family to be born in the United States with a U.S. citizenship.

William Maughon, Sr. and Nancy Maughon had three sons, William Jr., Peyton and Thomas. At some time during 1782, his first wife Nancy (1727-1782) died and he soon married Sarah Grant. In the midst of the horrifying Cherokee-American Wars, William Maughon Sr. and his family lived along the frontier near the fighting in North Carolina during 1784. According to census records in 1789, William Maughon Sr. and his family were still residing in North Hampton, North Carolina around the time the citizens voted to adopt the U.S. Constitution. North Carolina became a state six years after the Revolutionary War. This was one of the most tumultuous periods in American history. According to William Sr.'s last will and testament dated March 1795, he had acquired quite a profitable life for himself and his family. He is shown to have left ownership of at least 10 Negroes to his wife, Sarah as well as his home, his land, his money and other profitable assets.

When William Maughon, Jr. was born in 1750 his father and mother, William Sr., and Nancy, were both 23 years old. William Jr. had five sons and four daughters with Susannah Mildred "Millie" Mitchell Maughon between 1772 and 1790. During William Jr.'s life he served for seven years in the military and fought in the Revolutionary War. In addition to his time served he spent life as a cotton farmer. In 1794, Southerners like William Maughon Jr. heard talk of a new machine that could clean cotton faster than any man. This machine was Eli Whitney's cotton gin. William and his wife remained in North Carolina until their deaths.

William, Jr died on February 2, 1795 in Northampton, North Carolina at the age of 45. Although no known death date has been cited for Susannah, she is shown to be alive on the 1800 Federal Census. Nothing appears on her after that time. William, Jr. and Susannah were survived by their children, Salley Maughon born in 1772, Milley Maughon born in 1773, John Maughon born in 1775, Wiley Anjel Buchannan Maughon (1776-1861), Jessie Maughon born in 1777, Nathaniel Maughon born in 1778, Rebecca Maughon born in 1779, Edmund Maughon born in 1780, and Fanny Maughon born in 1790. There are no indicating records of death dates or marriage information for any of William, Jr.'s children with the exception of Wiley Anjel Buchannan Maughon who migrated farther south to Walton County, Georgia in the early 1800's.

Wiley Anjel Buchannan Maughon was born on July 5, 1776. He married Sarah Freeman Maughon on November 11, 1819 in Walton County, Georgia. Together they had 12 children in 22 years. Sarah Freeman Maughon was born in 1800 in Lincoln, Georgia, her father, Samuel Freeman, Sr. was 38 years old, and her mother, Susannah Allen Timmons Freeman was 38 years old. Sarah Freeman Maughon's father, Samuel Freeman, Sr. was born in Virginia in 1762. Soon after marrying his wife, Sarah Allen Timmons Freeman, the couple moved to Hickory Flat, Cherokee County, Georgia. According to the Georgia property tax records, Samuel Freeman, Sr. became a very wealthy farmer and owner of a very profitable plantation in Hickory Flat, Georgia.

Wiley Anjel Buchannan Maughon and Sarah Freeman Maughon was living in the 13 colonies at one of the most important turning points in American history—the signing of the Declaration of Independence. The Declaration of Independence was read for the first time on July 8, 1776 by a colonel in the Pennsylvania militia. Over the next month the scene was repeated in state houses and city squares across the colonies: New York City on July 9; Halifax, North Carolina, on July 22; and Savannah, Georgia, on August 10. Couriers delivered leaflets of the Declaration of Independence to as many cities in the thirteen colonies as they could.

By the 1820s, southern whites— especially farmers growing cotton—wanted more land. The problem was that the coveted lands belonged to members of the Five Civilized Tribes. The tribes—Cherokee, Chickasaw, Choctaw, Creek, and Seminole—had lived and hunted on the lands for generations. White settlers found an advocate in Andrew Jackson who strongly supported Native American removal. By 1828 with Jackson's ascendancy to the Oval Office, the groundwork was laid for the Indian Removal Act of 1830. With one swift signing of a pen, Native Americans saw their rights to stay on their lands effectively vanquished. By 1837, 46,000 Native Americans had been relocated to lands west of the Mississippi River. For whites, the Act made 25-million acres of land available for settlement. With the exception of the Seminoles who continued to fight for their lands in Florida, most of the Southern tribes were gone from the region. While Wiley Anjel Buchannan Maughon was a young man he held the occupation as a teacher in Walton County, Georgia. He taught for many years and was able to teach first hand these few monumental steps in our countries history. After years in the teaching profession he retired to a life of farming the rich fertile land that he had acquired as a result of the Removal Act. Although he witnessed these events first hand, he died on September 16, 1861 without bearing witness to seven of his nine sons and both of his sons in laws joining ranks with the Confederacy to fight for their beloved home and all that they held dear. His wife, Sarah, however, did witness the hardships and turmoil suffered by her family. She lived through the horrible news of her son, Mitchell Dooley Maughon being taken hostage by Union forces and held as prisoner of war and her son, Wiley Angel Buchannan, Jr. whom never returned home from the war. It was believed that he was killed while in battle against the Yankee forces. In 1863, Lincoln's Emancipation Proclamation was a bold document that freed enslaved African Americans while condemning the Confederacy. Initially, Lincoln was of two minds on slavery: Although he believed slavery "an unqualified evil," he also pledged not to interfere with states that practiced the "peculiar institution." However, with the outbreak of war, Lincoln's attitude shifted. He stated, "We must free the slaves or be ourselves subdued," thereby demonstrating a keen awareness that the federal government must take a stand. The Emancipation Proclamation freed 3.1 million enslaved African Americans. Lincoln went even further, inviting former enslaved individuals to take up arms against the Confederacy. Nearly 180,000 African Americans took him up on his offer. Lincoln paved the way for the eventual passage and ratification of the 13th Amendment in 1865 that abolished the institution of slavery entirely.

On November 15, 1864, three years into the American Civil War, Major General William Tecumseh Sherman of the Union Army cut the last telegraph wire that connected him to his superior officers, putting in motion a maneuver at odds with the set rules of war. Over the next five weeks, his army moved from Atlanta to the coast, employing a "scorched earth" campaign across Georgia: burning crops, killing livestock, and destroying any supplies that might support the Confederate Army. It took General Sherman and his troops 36 days to march the 300 miles from Atlanta to Savannah, Georgia. For civilians still in Georgia, mostly women and children who were left to fend for themselves, Sherman's March to the Sea was their worst nightmare. Entire cities were burned, railroads taken apart, homes demolished, and livestock shot down, "hunted as if they were rebels themselves," wrote Dolly Sumner Lunt, a resident of Covington, Georgia. Finally on December 22, General Sherman sent a telegram to President Lincoln: "I beg to present to you, as a Christmas gift, the city of Savannah." Without a doubt, Sarah Maughon experienced a society in turmoil and transition while living in Georgia during the 1870's in the midst of the Reconstruction Era. Her way of life, the only life she had ever known, changed severely and drastically during her old age. Census records indicate that she spent the few remaining years following the Civil War with her daughter, Elizabeth Maughon Wayne and her family. Records indicate that Wiley Anjel Buchannan Maughon's last will and testament did appoint Elizabeth's husband, Pvt. William P. Wayne as administrator of Wiley's estate and that he was also appointed to set aside money for both his and Sarah's funeral and burial expense. It was apparent that Wiley entrusted his daughter and her husband to care for his wife in her final days. On May 29, 1877, Sarah Freeman Maughon was laid to rest next to her husband, Wiley Anjel Buchannan Maughon in the Rest Haven Cemetery in Monroe, Walton County, Georgia.

Part Two

From Walton County, Georgia To Pike County, Alabama

FOLLOWING THE DEATH of their mother, Sarah Freeman Maughon in 1877, the Maughon children started to rebuild their lives and their families during the aftermath of the reconstruction era following the Civil War in 1865. Starting with the oldest of Wiley A.B. Maughon and Sarah Freeman Maughon's children was their son, Sidney Prince Maughon. Sidney Prince Maughon was born on April 9, 1821 in Walton County, Georgia to Sarah Freeman Maughon, age 21, and Wiley Anjel Buchannan Maughon, age 44.

Sidney Prince Maughon married Martha Ann Elizabeth Sansom on July 25, 1839 in his hometown. They had 13 children in 31 years. Sidney Prince Maughon saw service as a member of the Confederate States Army during the American Civil War. In 1862, Sidney enlisted with the 42nd Regiment Georgia Infantry Company C. He fought under the motto, "God Will Vindicate Us". The life of the Confederate soldier was one of constant battle—not only against the enemy, but also for food, pay, and clothing. It was not easy. Very different from the life on the farm that he had grown accustomed to. Times were hard and like so many men of that time, he wasn't prepared for such a change. He was a farmer, not a soldier.

The 42nd Infantry Regiment was assembled at Camp McDonald, Georgia during March of 1862, with men from Gwinnett, De Kalb, Newton, Walton, Fulton, and Calhoun counties. The regiment moved to Tennessee, then to Mississippi where it was attached to General Barton's Brigade in the Department of Mississippi and East Louisiana. The regiment fought at Chickasaw Bayou and Champion's Hill, and on July 4, 1863 was captured at Vicksburg. Exchanged and brigaded under General Stovall, the 42nd continued the fight in various battles from Missionary Ridge to Bentonville. In December, 1863 it contained 444 men and 394 arms, and in November, 1864 there were 345 present for duty. The regiment surrendered with the Army of Tennessee with 5 officers and 126 men. Its field officers were Colonel Robert J. Henderson, Lieutenant Colonels W.H. Hulsey and Robert F. Maddox, and Major Lovick P. Thomas.

Sidney Prince Maughon and Martha Ann Sansom Maughon's children include: Manerva Maughon Green who was born on September 1, 1840 in Auburn, Georgia. Her father, Sidney, was 19 and her mother, Martha was 16. She married John H. Green in 1861. Together they had six children in 13 years. She died on July 30, 1910 in her hometown at the age of 69 and was buried there alongside her husband. Manerva's husband, John worked throughout his life as a farm laborer to support his family. Sarah Maughon Stanley was born in 1842 in Auburn, Georgia her father, Sidney was 21 and her mother, Martha was 18. She had one daughter with John Thomas Stanley in 1865. She died on February 23, 1891, at the age of 49, and was buried in Collinsville, Alabama. Sarah's husband John spent his life as a profitable cotton farmer. Franklin Maughon was born in 1845 in Auburn, Georgia, his father, Sidney, was 24 and his mother, Martha was 21. Franklin was a private from Georgia who fought for the Confederacy during the Civil War. No records indicate his death date, death place or his marital status. No records appear for him at all after the Civil War, Malendia Maughon was born in 1847 in Georgia, her father, Sidney, was 26, and her mother, Martha, was 23. She died on May 15, 1931, in Gwinnett, Georgia, at the age of 84. No records indicate her marital status or her death place or burial location. When Thomas C. "Bud" Maughon was born on May 25, 1849 in Georgia, his father, Sidney was 28 and his mother, Martha was 24. He married Belle Robinson

Maughon on November 10, 1878, in Gwinnett, Georgia. They had six children in 10 years. He died on March 11, 1906, in Atlanta, Georgia, at the age of 56, and was buried in Auburn, Georgia at the Appalachee Baptist Church Cemetery. Thomas spent his life working as a farmer. John W. B. Maughon was born in January 1850 in Auburn, Georgia, his father, Sidney, was 28 and his mother, Martha, was 25. He married Mary Octavia Etheridge Maughon in 1872 in Georgia. They had 11 children in 22 years. He died on July 4, 1913, in Winder, Georgia, at the age of 63 and was buried in his hometown in the Appalachee Baptist Church Cemetery. John also spent his life working as a farmer to support his family. Cicero Mitchell Maughon was born in September 1850 in Gwinnett, Georgia, his father, Sidney, was 29 and his mother, Martha was 26. He married Elizabeth Letitia "Bettie" Hill Maughon on September 3, 1874, in his hometown. They had seven children in 12 years. He died on April 2, 1920, in Atlanta, Georgia, at the age of 69, and was buried in Auburn, Georgia in the Appalachee Baptist Church Cemetery. Cicero also spent his life as a farmer. When James Wiley Buchanan Maughon was born on April 6, 1856, in Auburn, Georgia, his father, Sidney, was 34 and his mother, Martha, was 31. He had three children with Talulah J. Robinson Maughon and one child with Alice Missouri Page Maughon. He died on January 2, 1939, in Barrow, Georgia, at the age of 82, and was buried in his hometown at the Appalachee Baptist Church Cemetery. Throughout his lifetime, James Wiley Buchannan Maughon made a successful living as a farmer. Henry G Maughon was born in 1858 in Gwinnett, Georgia, his father, Sidney, was 37 and his mother, Martha, was 34. He married Josephine "Josie" Hill on January 25, 1880, in his hometown. They had two children during their marriage. He died in 1900 at the age of 42. He worked most of his life as a farmer. Sidney Tink Maughon was born on December 31, 1863, in Winder, Georgia, his father, Sidney, was 42 and his mother, Martha, was 39. He married Allie Thomas and they had one daughter together and both mother and child died during childbirth. He then married Agnes Chestine Dillard and they had three children together. He died on April 22, 1916, in his hometown at the age of 52, and was buried in Auburn, Georgia in the Appalachee Baptist Cemetery. He spent his life working as a merchant. Samuel T. Maughon was born in 1864 in Georgia, his father, Sidney, was 43 and his mother, Martha, was 40. No further records indicate his date of death or place of burial. He doesn't show up on census records after the age of 16. Mary Olivia Maughon Jordan was born on July 5, 1869, in Georgia, her father, Sidney, was 48, and her mother, Martha, was 45. She had five sons and two daughters with Howell Jackson Jordan between 1895 and 1909. She died on March 5, 1938, in Gwinnett, Georgia, at the age of 68, and was buried in Auburn, Georgia. She and her husband Howell Jackson Jordan are buried at the Appalachee Baptist Church Cemetery. Howell Jackson Jordan spent his life working as a farmer.

Wiley Anjel Buchannan Maughon and Sarah Freeman Maughon's second child, William A. Maughon was born on September 6, 1822, in Georgia, his father, Wiley, was 46 and his mother, Sarah, was 22. He married Emily A. Barrett Maughon on August 2, 1842, in Walton, Georgia. They had five children in 19 years. He died on February 5, 1899, having lived a long life of 76 years. He was laid to rest at the Rest Haven Cemetery in Monroe, Walton County, Georgia. Corporal William A, Maughon joined the Confederate Army and served as 4th Corporal, Company G, 35th Regiment Georgia, Volunteer Infantry. During the American Civil War, the Confederacy required military service for all white males starting in the spring of 1862. He was living in Georgia in 1864 when the Confederacy raised a military draft. The drafted troops were often viewed with suspicion. Because they were mercenaries, volunteers feared they would desert in droves. Emily Barrett Maughon was only 19 years old when she married William on August 2, 1842, in her hometown. She died on June 17, 1894, in Walton, Georgia, at the age of 70, and was buried in Monroe, Georgia alongside her husband at the Rest Haven Cemetery in Walton, Georgia. Corporal William A. Maughon and Emily Barrett Maughon's children include: Jane Elizabeth Maughon Breedlove born on March 8, 1849 in Walton County, Georgia. Her father, William, was 26, and her mother, Emily, was 24 at the time of her birth. She had one son and five daughters with John W. Breedlove between 1872 and 1891. She died on February 1, 1931, in Richmond, Georgia, at the age of 81, and was buried in Walton, Georgia at the Shoal Creek Primitive Baptist Church Cemetery alongside her husband who died in 1921. John Breedlove spent his life working as a cotton farmer. Cotton played a major role in the success of the American South as well as its demise during the Civil War as many farmers of his time soon learned. Jane Elizabeth Maughon Breedlove and John Breeedlove were living in Georgia in 1849 when the cotton crop reigned as lifeblood to the state's economy. The second of William and Emily's children was a son named William A. B. Maughon. When William A.B. Maughon was born in 1851 in Georgia, his father, William, was 29 and his mother, Emily, was 27. He had one daughter with Mary Ann Nancy Elizabeth Smith Maughon in 1891. He died in 1891 within a few months of his daughter's birth in his hometown at the age of 40, and was buried in Monroe, Georgia at the Rest Haven Cemetery. After his death, Nancy married Thomas Martin Still who was a successful restaurant owner in downtown Monroe, Georgia. She had ten children with Thomas Martin Still. She died on January 3, 1963, in Fulton, Georgia, at the age of 91, and was buried in Loganville, Georgia at the Sharon Baptist Church Cemetery. William and Emily's third child was a daughter named Savannah Seleta "Vannie" Maughon Greene. Vannie was born on April 4, 1857 in Walton County, Georgia. Vannie was married to Anthony Greene. She died January 5, 1933 in Winder, Barrow, Georgia. Vannie is buried at the Rest Haven Cemetery in Walton County alongside her husband. No other records indicate their marriage date, whether or not they had any children or Anthony's occupation. William and Emily's fourth child is a daughter named Mary C. Maughon. When Mary C. Maughon was born in 1867 in Georgia, her father, William, was 45, and her mother, Emily, was 43. Mary never married. She was buried in Monroe, Georgia at the Rest Haven Cemetery. Her cemetery marker bears no death date. Census records indicate that she lived with other family members throughout her lifetime. The last record indicates that she was living with her niece and nephew, Fannie Bell Maughon Wood and Fred Wood in Winder, Georgia at the age of 75. Although it is unclear, but entirely possible the government programs started by the first "New Deal" in 1933 may have assisted Mary C. Maughon. By the spring of 1933, working class and rural Americans were tightly in the grip of the Great Depression. Forty percent of the nation's banks failed between 1929 and 1933, and almost 4-million manufacturing jobs were lost as consumption and production became locked in a downward spiral. The first "New Deal" created by President Franklin Roosevelt and his cabinet was aimed at providing relief and recovery to those hit hardest by the depressed economy. A farmer wrote in her diary in 1933 about the impact of the "New Deal" in rural areas: "Well, the national farm strike ... set for May 13 has been postponed, for which we are all thankful. They came to that decision after Roosevelt signed the farm bill, which makes it possible for the loan companies to refinance mortgages. ... Well, it gives us more courage to go on. We had about given up ever trying to keep up anymore." The youngest child of William and Emily Maughon was a son named Fredric George Maughon. Fredric George Maughon was born on May 23, 1868, in Walton, Georgia, his father, William, was 45 and his mother, Emily, was 43. He had one son and two daughters with Ella Harris Maughon between 1895 and 1910. He died on March 5, 1921, in Monroe, Georgia, at the age of 52, and was buried in the Rest Haven Cemetery. At the turn of the 20th century, textile manufacturing was one of the biggest industries in Georgia, employing thousands of men, women, and children. He was known to have spent his life working as a farmer to support his family. For those involved in the textile industry in Georgia at the turn of the 20th century, the mill regulated every aspect of life. Mill villages popped up throughout the state, where company-owned homes were situated around the factories. By 1910, more than 27,000 people reported employment at one of the 116 textile mills in the state, most of them living in company housing. Working in the mill was a family affair: fathers, mothers, and children could all take a job. During the peak of the textile industry in Georgia, around 25 percent of the employees were under the age of 16. Working in the mill was dangerous and tedious. Children were most often the victims of accidents, but adults were also susceptible to getting caught in machines or developing respiratory problems. New unmanned machinery, combined with new labor laws, forced the closure of many mill villages as the state moved into a more machine-driven industry. When the First World War began in 1914, the United States remained neutral. Despite this, German U-boats attacked U.S. merchant vessels and declared "unrestricted warfare against all ships" entering the war zone. Three years, into the conflict, President Woodrow Wilson stood in front of the U.S. Congress on April 2, 1917, and asked for a declaration of war, explaining that the United States must "exert all its power and employ all its resources" to end the First World War. Congress conceded. Thousands of Americans flocked to recruitment stations, eager to "do their bit" to defeat the enemy. Within nine months, 175,000 American soldiers were stationed along the Western Front, prepared to take on the Central Powers. While some Americans criticized President Wilson for going back on his promise to remain neutral, most eagerly put their backs into the war effort, supporting the four and a half million American soldiers who served in Western Europe. After years of neutrality, the United States officially declared war on Germany on April 6, 1917, providing much needed manpower and financial aid to the Allied cause. The textile mills weren't the only things changing times for the Maughon Family. A new generation was fast approaching. The olden days were fading fast. Wiley Anjel Buchannan Maughon and Sarah Freeman Maughon's third child was a son named Payton. Payton C. Maughon was born in 1823 in Walton, Georgia, his father, Wiley, was 47 and his mother, Sarah, was 23. He married Sarah E. Raines Maughon on December 2, 1845, in his hometown. They had nine children in 22 years. He died on June 25, 1900, in Walton, Georgia, having lived a long life of 77 years. No records have indicated where he and wife, Sarah are buried. Their children include their first born, Wiley Maughon born in 1846 in Walton County, Georgia. No records have been found to indicate his death date, death place, marital status or place of burial. Payton and Sarah's second born child was a daughter named Sarah Maughon McIntosh. Sarah Maughon McIntosh was born in October 1848 in Walton, Georgia, her father, Payton, was 25, and her mother, Sarah, was 19. She married David McIntosh on May 21, 1876, in her hometown. Her husband, Pvt. David McIntosh served in the 42nd Georgia Infantry Regiment Company H during the Civil War. After returning home from the war, he spent the rest of his life as a farmer. No records indicate where he or Sarah is buried. However, records do indicate that she is still alive at the age of 62 in 1910 and that he died on February 4, 1952 at the age of 105. The third child of Payton C. and Sarah Maughon was a daughter named Elizabeth L. Maughon. When Elizabeth L Maughon was born in April 1850 in Georgia, her father, Payton, was 27, and her mother, Sarah, was 21. She had one son with Augustus McCluskia "Gus" Maughon in 1880. She died in 1920 at the age of 70. Census records indicate that she was living with her mother in 1920. Both she and her mother died during that same year. Records do not indicate where she is buried. The third child of Payton C. and Sarah was a son named William Maughon. William Maughon was born in 1854 in Walton, Georgia, his father, Payton, was 31 and his mother, Sarah, was 25. He died in 1930 at the age of 76. No records indicate his place of burial or his marital status. The fifth child of Payton C. and Sarah was a son named Fredrick "Fred" Maughon. When Fredrick "Fred" Maughon was born on December 7, 1855, in Walton, Georgia, his father, Payton, was 32 and his mother, Sarah, was 26. He married Victoria E "Vickie" Patterson Maughon on January 25, 1891, in Cullman, Alabama. They had seven children in 14 years. He died on September 19, 1923, at the age of 67, and was buried in Hamlin, Texas. Records do not indicate a specific cemetery where he is buried. His wife, Vickie died in 1952 and was buried at the Circle View Cemetery in Walton County, Georgia. During the Great Depression, Victoria E. "Vickie" Patterson Maughon likely faced hardships like joblessness and scant resources while living in Fort Worth, Texas in 1936. October 24, 1929, was one of the darkest days in American history. On Black Tuesday, the hopeful, prosperity of the Roaring Twenties came to an abrupt end when the stock market crashed. Suddenly, the United States, and the world with it, was propelled into the Great Depression. Americans began withdrawing their money from banks, causing them to fail. Industrial production came to a standstill and unemployment skyrocketed. Unable to pay their bills, hundreds of thousands of Americans became homeless. By 1933, 15 million were without work and almost half of all U.S. banks had shuttered. To make matters worse, a historic drought caused widespread farmland erosion across the Prairie, precipitating the Dust Bowl. The "only thing we have to fear is fear itself" declared incoming President Franklin D. Roosevelt during his 1933 inauguration. Immediately he set to work rebuilding the country. Through a series of federal programs, he launched the New Deal, which revived banks, created millions of jobs, and helped Americans from going hungry. Slowly, the economy picked up, and with the outbreak of World War II in 1939, factories across the United States kicked into high gear, propelling the country out of the worst economic depression in its history. Payton C. and Sarah's sixth child was a son, his name was William. William was born in 1856 and died at the age of 4 in 1860. No records indicate where he is buried or the cause of his death. Payton C. and Sarah's seventh child was a child named Payton M. Maughon. The last record of Payton M. shows him working in a Gris Mill in 1880 at the age of 22 years old. His home is listed as Broken Arrow, Walton County, Georgia. No records indicate his marital status, his date or place of burial or death. Payton C. and Sarah's eighth child was a daughter named Martha Leanna "Anner" Maughon Norris. Martha Leanna "Anner" Maughon Norris was born on April 24, 1866, in Walton, Georgia, her father, Payton, was 43, and her mother, Sarah, was 37. She married Marion Luscious Edgar Norris in 1890. They had 11 children in 13 years. She died on December 16, 1939, in De Kalb, Georgia, at the age of 73, and was buried alongside her husband in Stone Mountain, Georgia. Marion L.E. Norris worked as a farmer to provide for his family. Martha Leanna "Anner" Maughon Norris of Broken Arrow, Georgia may have eagerly read the daily news hoping to hear more about Dr. Barnum Brown's fantastic fossil discoveries in 1900. At the turn of the 20th century, one man's love for discovery led him to become a world-famous fossil hunter. Dr. Barnum Brown came from humble beginnings, but his interest in archaeology would lead him to world-renowned success. After his outstanding work as a student at University of Kansas, Dr. Brown was offered a spot on a fossil dig that was operated by the American Museum of Natural History. He was soon hired as a field assistant for the museum, and eventually became the curator over a massive collection of dinosaur fossils that he had found himself. While participating in a dig in Hell Creek, Montana, in 1902, he located "bones of a large Carnivorous Dinosaur. . . .[He had] never seen anything like it from the Cretaceous." Dr. Brown had, in fact, discovered the first skeleton of a Tyrannosaurus rex. Over the next few decades he made several more significant discoveries. Dr. Brown's work made him a kind of scientific celebrity, and people flocked to see both him and the fossils he had unearthed. During one of his earlier digs, Dr. Brown discovered a shepherd's hut that was entirely made from fossils. This discovery was on August 9, 1934. Dr. Brown's worldwide travels gave him important geographic information, which he provided to the U.S. government during World War II. Dr. Brown's knowledge was sought after for several projects, including the dinosaur sequence in Walt Disney's film Fantasia. Payton C. and Sarah's ninth child was a daughter named Janie Maughon. Janie was born in 1868 and records show that she died in 1870 at the age of two years old. No records indicate the cause of death or where she is buried.

Wiley A.B. Maughon and Sarah Freeman Maughon's fourth child was a son named Francis Marion Maughon. Francis Marion Maughon was born on November 28, 1825, in Walton, Georgia, his father, Wiley, was 49 and his mother, Sarah, was 25. He married Selatta Barrett Maughon on June 16, 1846, in his hometown. They had nine children in 19 years. He died on June 22, 1905, in Barrow, Georgia, having lived a long life of 79 years, and was buried in Good Hope, Georgia alongside his wife. During Francis Marion's life he joined the Confederate forces to fight in the Civil War. He enlisted in on 23 Mar 1862.Mustered out on 16 Nov 1862 at Richmond, VA., enlisted in Company G, Georgia 42nd Infantry Regiment on 23 Sep 1863. During the American Civil War, the sheer volume of wounded soldiers forced doctors and nurses to develop life-saving medical techniques. Francis Marion Maughon was a soldier who likely required medical treatment. The vast majority of deaths during the American Civil War were not on the battlefield; they were caused by disease. In 1861 germ theory did not exist, the root of infection remained a mystery, and medical training was crude. Little advancements had been made in the field since the American Revolution; some physicians still championed medieval methods of bloodletting, purging, and blistering to rebalance the body's humors. However, development in weaponry, namely faster, more accurate rifles and shells killed hundreds of thousands and left many more badly wounded. Thus the war forced doctors and nurses to rethink medical treatments, as tens of thousands of soldiers flooded the ill-equipped field hospitals. The sheer volume of injured men prompted rapid amputations. By 1865, a surgeon could remove a limb in six minutes flat. Anesthetics were common—chloroform and ether were given to patients, along with morphine for the pain. Ambulance service also was born during the Civil War. The fallen were gathered from the field, their wounds wrapped up, and they were shuttled to battle-side hospitals. But for many, these advancements in techniques and sanitation came too little too late—upwards of 500,000 Americans died from disease and infection before the war's end. Advancements in military weapons made the American Civil War a conflict of unparalleled carnage. Francis Marion Maughon likely used new weapons when he fought in the American Civil War. During the American Civil War, new weaponry revolutionized battle. The repeating rifle with Minié balls that allowed soldiers to fire seven rounds in 30 seconds without reloading replaced the musket. The repeating rifle increased accuracy, extending the firing range from 80 yards to 1,000. Thus forces were spaced further apart on the battlefield and to protect themselves built extensive fortifications and trenches. Hand grenades and land mines also came into use during the war. However, the new explosives were finicky—sometimes Confederate soldiers used blankets to catch the incoming explosives and simply tossed them back to Union lines, where they exploded. From the skies, passenger balloons spied on enemy lines and from below, Confederate submarines attacked ironclad ships enforcing the Union blockade. Unfortunately, technological advancements outpaced medical innovation. The wounds caused by these new weapons were often deadly. In battle, modernized weapons proved harrowing. The sheer scale of fatalities and injuries was unmatched and, today, the Civil War remains the deadliest conflict in American history. Prior to the Civil War, Francis Marion returned home to Walton County, Georgia to spend the remainder of his life as a farmer in order to support his family. Francis Marion and Selatta's first child was a son named, James M. Maughon. When James M Maughon was born on August 12, 1847, in Walton, Georgia, his father, Francis, was 21 and his mother, Selatta, was 21. He died as a child at the age of 12 on April 24, 1859, in Georgia, and was buried in Good Hope, Georgia at the Carlton Family Cemetery. Francis Marion and Selatta's second child was a son named Augustus McCluskia "Gus" Maughon. Augustus McCluskia "Gus" Maughon was born on February 28, 1849, in Georgia, his father, Francis, was 23 and his mother, Selatta was 22. He had one son with Elizabeth L Maughon in 1880. Gus spent his life as a farmer. He died on October 15, 1926, in his hometown at the age of 77, and was buried in Good Hope, Georgia at the Carlton Family Cemetery. The third child of Francis Marion and Selatta Maughon was a son named George Malcom Maughon. George Malcom Maughon was born on September 5, 1851, in Walton, Georgia, his father, Francis, was 25 and his mother, Selatta was 25. He married Susan Maughon in 1900. They had eight children in 27 years. George spent his life working as a farmer. He died on January 20, 1918, in his hometown at the age of 66, and was buried in Good Hope, Georgia at the Carlton Family Cemetery. The fourth child of Francis Marion and Selatta Maughon was a daughter named Amanda Wylie Maughon. Amanda Wylie Maughon was born on October 13, 1853, in Walton, Georgia, her father, Francis, was 27, and her mother, Selatta was 27. She worked most of her life as a dress maker. She died on November 12, 1902, in Wellington, Georgia, at the age of 49, and was buried in Good Hope, Georgia at the Carlton Family Cemetery. The fifth child of Francis Marion and Selatta Maughon was a son named Richard Barrett "Turner" Maughon. When Richard Barrett "Turner" Maughon was born on March 30, 1856, in Walton, Georgia, his father, Francis, was 30 and his mother, Selatta, was 29. He married Martha Ophelia Malcom on December 24, 1879, in his hometown. They had six children in 13 years. Richard worked as a farmer to support his family. He died on December 8, 1938, in Fulton, Georgia, at the age of 82, and was buried in Good Hope, Georgia at the Carlton Family Cemetery. The sixth child of Francis Marion and Selatta Maughon was a son named William Aaron "Jack" Maughon. William Aaron "Jack" Maughon was born on December 31, 1860, in Georgia, his father, Francis, was 35 and his mother, Selatta was 34. He married Hattie Lee Lewis Maughon on December 28, 1892, in Morgan, Georgia. They had one child during their marriage. Jack spent his life working as a farmer. He died on January 2, 1937, in Walton, Georgia, at the age of 76, and was buried in Bostwick, Georgia at the Bostwick Cemetery. The seventh child of Francis Marion and Selatta Maughon was a son named John Thrasher "Pomp" Maughon. John Thrasher "Pomp" Maughon was born in 1863 in Walton, Georgia, his father, Francis, was 38 and his mother, Selatta was 37. He married Leola Matilda Mitchem in 1894. They had three children in 15 years. Pomp worked as a farmer to support his family. He died on November 1, 1926, in his hometown at the age of 63, and was buried in Good Hope, Georgia at the Carlton Family Cemetery. The eighth child of Francis Marion and Selatta Maughon was a son named Henry Green "Sam" Maughon. Henry Green "Sam" Maughon was born on May 7, 1864, in Georgia, his father, Francis, was 38 and his mother, Selatta was 38. Although Sam was never married, he did work as a farmer to support himself. He died on March 18, 1925, in Bostwick, Georgia, at the age of 60, and was buried in Good Hope, Georgia at the Carlton Family Cemetery. The ninth and youngest child of Francis Marion and Selatta Maughon was a daughter named Sallie Sarah Maughon. When Sallie Sarah J Maughon was born in May 1867 in Georgia, her father, Francis, was 41, and her mother, Selatta was 41. Although Sallie never married, she did work as a dressmaker to help support herself. She died on May 23, 1956, in Fulton, Georgia, at the age of 89, and was buried in Good Hope, Georgia at the Carlton Family Cemetery.

Wiley A.B. Maughon and Sarah Freeman Maughon's fifth child was a daughter named Martha Maughon Snow. Martha Maughon Snow was born on July 8, 1827, in Walton, Georgia, her father, Wiley, was 51, and her mother, Sarah was 27. She married Samuel G. Snow on July 24, 1845, in her hometown. They had two children during their marriage. She died on January 21, 1908, in Walton, Georgia, having lived a long life of 80 years. She was buried at the Rest Haven Cemetery. Her husband Samuel died sometime between 1850 and 1860. No records indicate where he is buried or cause of death. The sixth child of Wiley A.B. Maughon and Sarah Freeman Maughon was a son named Wiley A.B. Maughon, Jr. Wiley A.B., Jr. was born in 1830 in Georgia, his father, Wiley, was 54 and his mother, Sarah, was 30. He joined the Confederate forces to fight in the Civil War. Wiley A.B., Jr. was in the Army of Virginia; He was supposedly captured and died in prison. He never returned home from the War. He died in 1864 in his hometown at the age of 34.

By 1800 cotton was king. The Deep South in the United States supplied most of the world's cotton—in booming British factories, it was spun into fabric then sold around the empire. Farmers across the region were producing larger harvests than ever before thanks to the cotton gin, and more cotton required more labor. Four million enslaved African Americans lived in the South by 1850, most toiling on plantations 16 hours a day, pruning, watering, and harvesting. Small farms with few or no slaves also tried their hand at the crop, but the 1 percent of families in the South who owned more than 100 slaves dominated wealth and power in the region. They devoted their days to entertaining and politics, sending their children to elite schools in the North and abroad. At the onset of the American Civil War, cotton would financially sustain Confederate troops and even play into war strategy. By war's end, the cotton industry and the American South were transformed forever. Cotton played a major role in the success of the American South as well as its demise during the Civil War. Wiley A. B. Maughon, Jr. was living in Georgia in 1830 when the cotton crop reigned as lifeblood to the state's economy. Prior to the Civil War there was millions of acres up for grabs in the 19th century, Georgia implemented a lottery system to encourage settlement. The Maughon family lived in Georgia in 1830, a time when the state redistributed about 75 percent of its land. Hundreds of men, widows, and orphans over the age of 18 rushed to stake their claims when millions of acres in Georgia—land taken from Cherokee and Creek tribes—opened up for settlement in 1805 to white pioneers. Tickets representing the hopeful landowners were pulled from barrels at crowded public drawings. About 20 percent of applicants won, taking home between tracts that were 40 to 490-acres, some rich with gold. Given that thousands of Cherokee and Creek Native Americans had been forcibly removed from their homelands for the lotteries, the system was met with resistance. Their protests were taken all the way to the Supreme Court that ruled in favor of protecting native lands in 1832. But backed by the U.S. Army, U.S. President Andrew Jackson ignored the mandate and relocated the tribes to reservations out West. After eight lotteries over the course of 28 years, 75 percent of the state's land had been redistributed before the system was disbanded in 1833. According to land lottery records found in the archives, much of the land settled by the Maughon Family was obtained thru these lotteries.

    The seventh child of Wiley A.B. and Sarah Freeman Maughon was a daughter named Elizabeth Maughon Wayne. When Elizabeth Maughon

Wayne was born on May 31, 1831, in Walton, Georgia, her father, Wiley, was 54, and her mother, Sarah, was 31. She married Pvt. William Parks Wayne in 1852 in her hometown. They had seven children in 24 years. Her husband, Pvt. William Parks Wayne served in the Civil War in Company B 23rd Battalion Georgia Infantry. After returning home from the war, he worked as a farmer and blacksmith to support his family. In 1870, Pvt. William Parks Wayne may have witnessed or experienced political discrimination while living in Monroe, Georgia after ratification of the 15th Amendment. The 15th Amendment outlawed racial discrimination at the election polls, but white leaders in the South ignored the Constitution. Pvt. William Parks Wayne died on October 11, 1900. Elizabeth Maughon Wayne died on December 23, 1907, in Walton, Georgia, having lived a long life of 76 years. She and her husband are buried at the Rest Haven Cemetery in Walton County, Georgia.

Wiley A.B. Maughon and Sarah Freeman Maughon's eighth child was a son named Mitchell Dooley Maughon. When Mitchell Dooley Maughon was born on March 24, 1833 in Walton County, Georgia, his father, Wiley was 56 and his mother, Sarah was 33. Pvt. Mitchell Dooley Maughon first entered service to serve in the American Civil War on June 20, 1861 at Arkadelphia, Arkansas. He served in the 2nd Arkansas Battery, Robert's Battery, and continued until June 1865. He was captured as prisoner on June 27, 1863 at Shelbyville, Tennessee and was held at Camp Douglas in Chicago, Illinois. Camp Douglas located in Chicago, Illinois, is sometimes described as "The North's Andersonville," was one of the largest Union Army prisoner-of-war camps for Confederate soldiers taken prisoner during the American Civil War. Based south of the city on the prairie, it was also used as a training and detention camp for Union soldiers. The Union Army first used the camp in 1861 as an organizational and training camp for volunteer regiments. It became a prisoner-of-war camp in early 1862. Later in 1862 the Union Army again used Camp Douglas as a training camp. In the fall of 1862, the Union Army used the facility as a detention camp for paroled Confederate prisoners.

Camp Douglas became a permanent prisoner-of-war camp from January 1863 to the end of the war in May 1865. The high mortality rate can be attributed to several factors: overcrowding, unhealthy living conditions, ineffective medical treatment, inadequate food supply, and brutality. The war lasted longer than expected, resulting in more prisoners than anticipated. By late 1862 there were 8,962 prisoners in the camp with fewer than 900 guards. Over 200 prisoners were crowded in to barracks averaging 70 feet by 25 feet. As the number increased, tents were erected to house them, with little protection against below zero winds. Huge latrines were left open, so rain washed raw sewage into the drinking water supply. Wooden floors were removed to discourage tunneling, so vermin infected the dirt floors. Rats and mice were commonplace. Some unnamed inmates recollecting the camp 37 years later said that they raised the kitchen floor to catch "big gray rats" which were made into rat pies. When cholera and a smallpox epidemic erupted, free medicine sent by the South was withheld as contraband of war. Food rations were restricted, partly to cut costs and partly as retaliation for Southern victories. When control of the camp was finally passed to the Chicago Police department, medical supplies were cut off and food severely restricted. In the summer and fall of 1865, the camp served as a mustering out point for Union Army volunteer regiments. The camp was dismantled and the movable property was sold off late in the year. The land was eventually sold-off and developed.

In the aftermath of the war, Camp Douglas eventually came to be noted for its poor conditions and death rate of about seventeen percent; although it is possible a higher rate occurred. Some 6,000 Confederate prisoners were known to be re-interred from the camp cemetery to a mass grave at Oak Woods Cemetery after the war.

Mitchell Dooley Maughon was later paroled on June 20, 1865. The two long hard years that he was held proved to be extremely difficult. He nearly starved to death and suffered inhumane hardships that one can only imagine. It is noted that he was wounded twice at Shelbyville, Tennessee and fought battles at Shiloh and Murfreesboro. After returning home, he continued to suffer long-term side effects of the horrible ordeal. Mitchell Dooley Maughon moved to Brundidge, Pike County, Alabama in 1868. He married Rebecca Orpah Flowers Maughon on April 2, 1891 in Troy, Pike County, Alabama. He and Orpah didn't have any children together. When he died his estate was willed to Orpah and upon her death it was left to Mitchell's niece, Mrs. Mitchell D. Maughon Johnston of Brundidge, Alabama. She cared both for both her uncle Mitchell and Aunt Orpah in their later years. Mitchell owned a large farm of 200 acres located four miles south west of Brundidge, Alabama. The farm was always under high cultivation and faired extremely well. He died on August 17, 1911, in Pike County, Alabama after having lived a long life of 78 years. He was buried in Brundidge, Alabama at the Union Springs Primitive Baptist Church where he served as deacon for many years and as school master after returning home from the war. After Mitchell's death, Orpah married Judge Nelson Hurston. Rebecca Orpah Flowers Maughon was born on June 10, 1858 and raised in Brundidge, Pike County, Alabama.

Orpah Flowers Maughon Hurston died on January 6, 1922 and is also buried at Union Springs Primitive Baptist Church next to her second husband, Judge Nelson Hurston. Orpah was the daughter of Wingate and Malatha Pate Flowers who were both citizens of Brundidge, Alabama.

The ninth child of Wiley A.B. Maughon and Sarah Freeman Maughon was a daughter named Rebecca Jane Maughon Caldwell. Rebecca Jane Maughon Caldwell was born on August 30, 1835, in Monroe, Georgia, her father, Wiley, was 59, and her mother, Sarah, was 35. She married Corp. James Monroe Caldwell on June 5, 1856, in Walton, Georgia. They had nine children in 21 years. Corp. James Monroe Caldwell enlisted in Company G, 9th Georgia Infantry Regiment. He joined the Confederate troops to fight on June 12, 1861 and was promoted to full corporal and mustered out on May 19, 1865 in Thomasville, Georgia. James Monroe spent his remaining years after the Civil War working as a painter to support his family. He died on June 9, 1899 in Walton County, Georgia. She died on March 9, 1908, in her hometown at the age of 72, and was buried at the Rest Haven Cemetery in Walton County, Georgia alongside her husband.

The tenth child born to Wiley A.B. and Sarah Freeman Maughon was a son named John Angle Maughon. Pvt. John Angle Maughon was born on August 15, 1837, in Walton, Georgia, his father, Wiley, was 61 and his mother, Sarah was 37. He had two sons and three daughters with his first wife, Mary E. Dunford Maughon. John Angle Maughon moved from Walton County, Georgia sometime around 1860 to Coffee County, Alabama and married his first wife, Mary Dunford. In April 1861, John Angle Maughon enlisted in the Confederate Army as a Private in the 33rd Alabama Regiment Company K and continued until the close of war. He was listed as at home during the surrender due to injuries received at New Hope Church in Clintonville, Coffee County, Alabama and was consequently paroled at that time.

The 33rd Regiment Alabama Infantry was an infantry unit from Alabama that served in the Confederate States Army during the U.S. Civil War. Recruited from the southeastern counties of Butler, Dale, Coffee, Covington, Russell and Montgomery, it saw extensive service with the Confederate Army of Tennessee before being nearly annihilated at the Battle of Franklin in 1864. Survivors from the regiment would continue to serve until the final capitulation of General Joseph Johnston in North Carolina in 1865, though the 33rd had been combined with remnants of three other regiments prior to the surrender.

In addition to the counties named above, the 33rd Alabama drew recruits from three modern Alabama counties that did not yet exist in 1862: Geneva County, which was then a part of Dale and Coffee counties; Crenshaw County, which would be formed from Covington and other nearby counties after the war; and Houston County, which then formed a part of Dale and Henry Counties.

For much of its service, the 33rd fought under the "Stonewall of the West:" Major General Patrick Cleburne, an Irish-born officer whom General Robert E. Lee once referred to as "a meteor shining from a clouded sky" for his battlefield prowls. Though it took horrifying losses at the Battle of Perryville (where it suffered eighty-two percent casualties) and at Franklin (where it lost two-thirds of its numbers), it held together until the final Carolina Campaign in 1865. One debatable fact uncovered seems to imply that Alabama was a divided state during the American Civil War, with a sizable number of north Alabamians fighting for the Union.

Alabama's pivotal role in the American Civil War was reflected in the choice of Montgomery as the first capital of the Confederacy when Alabama seceded from the Union on January 11, 1861. Secession was not unanimous; some residents of north Alabama resisted secession and fought for the Union Army. Initially, Alabama Confederates successfully seized all federal forts in its territories, but Union forces quickly captured North Alabama and in 1864 blockaded Mobile Bay to prevent the shipment of supplies to Confederate troops. About 100,000 white men served in the Confederate militia, which suffered from a lack of uniforms, food, and weapons. Slaves were also pressed into military duty to dig trenches, cook, launder, care for animals, and grade roads, though many fled to freedom under the cover of Union forces. At home, women coped with limited medical supplies to treat the wounded, as well as food shortages. Montgomery finally surrendered to the Union on April 12, 1865.

John Angle Maughon and Mary Dunford Maughon's first child was a daughter named Sarah Maughon. Sarah was born in 1864. No records surfaced on Sarah after the age of 16 in 1880 living in Eufaula, Alabama.

In 1869, John Angle and Mary Dunford Maughon had a son named John W. Maughon. John W. Maughon married Hattie Brown in Eufaula, Alabama in 1889. No records appear for either of them after this time. No burial year or place was found for them. In 1870, John Angle and Mary Dunford Maughon had a daughter named Mary "Mattie" Maughon. Mattie married James William Benjamin Matthews in Ozark, Alabama on August 15, 1890. Mattie and James W.B. Matthews had two children together, Ruth B. Matthews in December 1891 and Loys Vaden Matthews in December 1894. No records appear for Ruth or Mattie after 1920. No record of death or marriage on Ruth appears. Loys Vaden Matthews marries Mildred Matthews but no records indicate if they had any children. Loys Vaden owned and operated a jewelry store located on Union Street in downtown Ozark, Alabama. Loys Vaden and Mildred are both buried at the Union Cemetery in Ozark, Alabama. In 1873, John Angle Maughon and Mary Dunford Maughon had a son named Robert Maughon. No records appear for him after 1880 in Eufaula, Alabama. In 1875, John Angle Maughon and Mary Dunford Maughon had a daughter named Susie Maughon. No records appear for her either after 1880 in Eufaula, Alabama.

John Angle Maughon married Emily Catherine Amos Black on May 31, 1885 following the death of his first wife, Mary Dunford Maughon in 1882.

John Angle Maughon then moved to Pike County, Alabama permanently sometime between 1882 and 1885. Census records do not indicate that the first five children of John Angle Maughon also made the move with him to Pike County, Alabama. The later records indicate that they were still residing in Eufaula, Alabama. Emily Catherine Maughon's first husband, Henry Black is shown to have died in early 1885. She was pregnant with her second child by Henry Black at the time. Her two children by Henry Back were both sons, Captain Daniel Belve Black and William Edgar Black. William Edgar Black was born January 07, 1885. Shortly after the death of her first husband Henry, Emily Catherine married John Angle Maughon on May 31, 1885. John Angle raised both sons as his own. He and Emily had eight children of their own.

Captain Daniel Belve Black was born on March 5, 1883, in Pike County, Alabama, the son of Emily Catherine Amos Black and Henry Black. He had three sons and two daughters with his wife, Emily Allen Black between 1912 and 1930. Daniel Belve spent his life working as a farmer to support his family. He died on January 16, 1955 in Troy, Alabama at the age of 71, and was buried in Brundidge, Alabama alongside his wife Emily at Shady Grove Baptist Church.

Daniel and Emily Black's firstborn was a son named JT Black. When JT Black was born on October 12, 1912 in Pike County, Alabama his father, Captain Daniel Belve Black was 29 and his mother, Emily Allen Black was 22. He married Jean Mary Paul on July 16, 1953, in Virginia. No census records indicate if there were any children born unto this marriage. He died on January 23, 1979, in Decatur, Alabama, at the age of 66, and was buried in Brundidge, Alabama at the Shady Grove Baptist Cemetery.

Daniel and Emily's second child was a daughter named Estin B. Black. Estin was married to JD Flowers of the Tarentum Community in Brundidge, Alabama. Between 1935 and 1938 they had four daughters and four sons together, Ruth F. Flowers Carnley, Lounell Flowers Mobley, Estelle Flowers Napper, Judy Flowers, John David Flowers, Jerry Flowers, Jerome Flowers and Jerrell Flowers. Their children settled within the Tarentum Community and Coffee/Pike County area along with their families. JD and Estin Flowers are buried along with their children, Estelle, Lounell, and Jerry at Mt. Olive Assembly of God Church in Brundidge, Alabama.

Daniel and Emily Black's third born child was a daughter named Clyde Black Flowers. When Clyde Black Flowers was born on September 22, 1918 in Alabama, her father, Captain Daniel Belve Black was 35, and her mother, Emily Allen Black was 28. She married Albert David Flowers in September 1939 in Pike, Alabama. Together they had four children, Joyce Flowers Ferry, Evelyn Flowers Lott, Larry Flowers and Alvin Flowers. Clyde Black Flowers died on January 15, 2001 in Brundidge, Alabama, at the age of 82, and was buried at the Mt. Olive Assembly of God Church alongside her husband, Albert David Flowers who died August 29, 1988. Clyde and Albert's daughter, Evelyn is also buried at Mt. Olive Church cemetery.

Throughout the summer of 1936, the United States experienced one of the most devastating heatwaves in the nation's history. Clyde Black Flowers and her siblings experienced one of the worst heatwaves in North American history while living in Pike County, Alabama during the summer of 1936. For eight consecutive days in 1936, from July 7th to July 14th, the thermometer at Midway Airport in Chicago climbed above 100 degrees. About 200 deaths were attributed to the heatwave in the city, but Chicago was just one of many places where extremely hot weather caused havoc that summer. Across America, the heatwave was blamed for more than 5,000 deaths and the failure of crops in the nation's breadbasket. Several Midwestern and Plains states experienced record high average temperatures for the summer. Severe drought also accompanied the sweltering heat. This caused sharp increases in the price of staple foods during the Great Depression. A man from central Wisconsin described the situation in his area to the Milwaukee Journal on July 8th by saying, "We had 103 yesterday and no breeze and there's no let-up. Last week we had a little rain—just a trifle, just enough to settle the dust."

The fourth born child to Captain Daniel Belve and Emily Allen Black was their son, Hubert Black. When Hubert Black was born on July 9, 1927, in Pike County, Alabama, his father, Captain Daniel Belve, was 44 and his mother, Emily was 37. He was married on September 16, 1950 in Pike County, Alabama. He died in June 1986 in Jack, Alabama at the age of 58. Census records of that time do not indicate his wife's name or children's names or his place of burial.

The fifth child born to Captain Daniel Belve Black and Emily Allen Black was their son named CB Black. When CB Black was born on June 12, 1929, in Pike County, Alabama, his father, Captain Daniel Belve, was 46 and his mother, Emily was 39. His wife's name is Annie Black. He died on August 17, 2003 in New Brockton, Alabama at the age of 74, and was buried there at the New Brockton City Cemetery with his wife. Census records do not indicate the names of their children.

Emily Catherine Amos Black Maughon and her first husband, Henry Black's second child was a son named William Edgar Black. William Edgar Black was born on January 7, 1885, in Pike County, Alabama. He married Mary "Toodie" Goodson Black on January 18, 1907, in his hometown. They had seven children in 16 years.

William Edgar and Toodie's children include their firstborn, Henry Veto Black (1908-1996). Henry Veto married Blondell Brooks Black on June 17, 1928 and they had three sons which include: Paul Black, Ray Black, and Jackie Black. Henry and Blondell Black are buried at St. John Baptist Church Cemetery in the Tarentum Community in Brundidge, Alabama.

William Edgar and Toodie's second born child was a son who lived less than a year, Clyde Black (1911-1911). William and Edgar's third born child was a son named JK Black (1913-1986). JK Black married Eva Lou Connor Black on May 19, 1940. JK and Eva Lou spent their lives as well known and loved store proprietor's in the Tarentum Community. JK and Eva Lou Black are buried at St. John Baptist Church Cemetery in the Tarentum community.

Mary Catherine Black (1915-1915) was the fourth born child of William Edgar and Toodie who lived less than a year. Noah Black (1919-2007) was the fifth born child of William Edgar and Toodie Black. Noah married Grace Griswold Black on October 28, 1944. They had three sons, Randy Black, Noah Gene Black and Gary Black. Noah and Grace spent their lives as well known and loved store proprietor's in Brundidge, Alabama after Noah served our country during World War II.

The sixth born child of William Edgar and Toodie black was a son named Douglas Black (1921-1998). Records indicate that Douglas also served our country during World War II. The seventh born child of William Edgar and Toodie Black was their son, Cliff Black (1925-2018). Cliff married Helen Virginia Ward Black in March of 1968. Cliff and Virginia had two daughters, Donna Black Massey and Dale Black Wilder. Both Cliff and Virginia are buried at St. John Baptist Church Cemetery in the Tarentum Community.

William Edgar worked as a farmer to support his family. He died on March 24, 1963 in Brundidge, Alabama, at the age of 78. Both William Edgar and Toodie are buried at St. John Baptist Church Cemetery in the Tarentum Community.

When the United States declared war on Germany in 1917, William Edgar Black and his brother, Captain Daniel Belve Black was living in Tarentum, Alabama. After years of neutrality, the United States officially entered the war on April 6, 1917, providing much needed manpower and financial aid to the Allied cause. When the First World War began in 1914, the United States remained neutral. Despite this, German U-boats attacked U.S. merchant vessels and declared "unrestricted warfare against all ships" entering the war zone. Three years, into the conflict, President Woodrow Wilson stood in front of the U.S. Congress on April 2, 1917, and asked for a declaration of war, explaining that the United States must "exert all its power and employ all its resources" to end the First World War. Congress conceded. Thousands of Americans flocked to recruitment stations, eager to "do their bit" to defeat the enemy. Within nine months, 175,000 American soldiers were stationed along the Western Front, prepared to take on the Central Powers. While some Americans criticized President Wilson for going back on his promise to remain neutral, most eagerly put their backs into the war effort, supporting the four and a half million American soldiers who served in Western Europe. . On April 2, 1917, President Woodrow Wilson addressed the United States Congress, asking for a declaration of war. Four days later, the U.S. Senate voted: 82 for and 6 against. In the House of Representatives, the decision was endorsed again 373 votes to 50. On April 6, 1917, President Woodrow Wilson asked that "all officers, civil or military, of the United States exercise vigilance and zeal in the discharge of the duties incident to such a state of war." On June 26, 1917, just a few months after the U.S. officially joined the war, 14,000 U.S. infantrymen landed in France. They were immediately put through more combat training and, within a few months, were fighting on the Western Front. 1917. Enacted just a month after the U.S. declared war on Germany, the Selective Service Act required all males from the ages of 21 to 30 to register for military service. By the end of the war, half of the 4.8 million soldiers in the American military had been drafted. Census records indicate that William Edgar's brother, Captain Daniel Belve Black was indeed signed up for the enacted draft of World War I, as well as the draft for World War II. William Edgar Black was enlisted in the World War II draft as he wasn't old enough for the World War I draft. Without a doubt, the Black family has been an enormous contribution to the Brundidge and Tarentum area they have always been a pillar to our little area and a much loved family.

Pvt. John Angle Maughon and Emily Catherine Amos Maughon had eight children together. After the war John Angle devoted his time and life as a successful and much respected farmer. Their children include their first born daughter, Minnie Lee Maughon Shiver. When Minnie Lee Maughon Shiver was born in March 1889 in the Tennille community of Pike County, Alabama her father, Pvt. John Angle Maughon was 51, and her mother, Emily Catherine Amos Maughon was 26. She married Charlie Marion Shiver on February 14, 1908, in Pike County, Alabama. They had four children in 20 years. Minnie and Charlie's children include: Vonnie Lee Shiver Flowers who married Joe Tom Flowers, Woodrow Wilson Shiver who married Rose Mae Whittington Shiver, Evelyn C. Shiver Dickey who married Curtis Dickey and their fourth child named Charles Hubbert Shiver. Minnie Lee Maughon Shiver died on July 2, 1968, in Troy, Alabama, at the age of 79 and Charlie Marion died in 1977 at the age of 87. They are both buried at Hamilton Crossroads Church of Christ Cemetery in Brundidge, Alabama. For many decades the Shiver family has been a huge part of the Tennille/Hamilton Cross Roads community. Always much loved and highly respected for their contributions and hard work for the community.

Pvt. John Angle Maughon and Emily Catherine Amos Maughon's second born child was a daughter named Mitchell D. Maughon Johnston.

Mitchell D. Maughon Johnston was born on October 26, 1890 in Pike County, Alabama. Her father, Pvt. John Angle Maughon was 53 and her mother, Emily Catherine Maughon was 28. Mitchell D. Maughon Johnston married Matha "Mattie" Gilbert Johnston in 1909 at the age of 19. They had eight children in 22 years. Their children include: MD Johnston, Mary Kate Johnston, and Francis Johnston Jernigan who married Joseph Edward Jernigan, John Fred Johnston, Joe Ray Johnston, and Ruby Johnston Lyons who married James R. Lyons, Billie Johnston, and Jim Bob Johnston. Mitchell D. Maughon Johnston died on March 17, 1963 in Pike County, Alabama, at the age of 72, and was buried alongside her husband at the St. John Baptist Church Cemetery in Brundidge, Alabama.

Pvt. John Angle Maughon and Emily Catherine Maughon's third born child was a son named Rufus Daynor Maughon. When Rufus Daynor Maughon was born on September 12, 1893 in Pike County, Alabama his father, Pvt. John Angle Maughon was 56 and his mother, Emily was 31. He had one son and one daughter with Nelie Grace Wilson Maughon between 1920 and 1922. Their son, John Daynor Maughon lived for less than a year. He is buried next to his parents. Their daughter, Amanda Katherine Maughon Flowers married James Williams Flowers. They are also buried at St. John Baptist Cemetery. Rufus Daynor died on January 25, 1946, at the age of 52 and is buried at St. John Baptist Church in the Tarentum community alongside his wife. Rufus Daynor is fondly remembered by his nieces and nephews as "Uncle Dane".

Pvt. John Angle Maughon and Emily Catherine Maughon's fourth born child was a daughter named Cannie Maughon Wilson. When Cannie Maughon Wilson was born on October 17, 1895 in Alabama, her father, Pvt. John Angle Maughon was 58, and her mother, Emily Catherine Maughon, was 33. She married Frank Rainer Wilson on December 20, 1914, in Pike County, Alabama. They had two children during their marriage. Their children were Mae Wilson Fryer married to John Lude Fryer and Maureen Wilson Jackson married to John Hatcher "Bill" Jackson. Cannie Maughon Wilson died on February 12, 1982 in Brundidge, Alabama at the age of 86, and was buried there.

The fifth child born unto Pvt. John Angle Maughon and Emily

Catherine Maughon was a daughter named Patsy Maughon. When Patsy Maughon was born in February 1897 in Pike County, Alabama her father, Pvt.John Angle Maughon was 59, and her mother, Emily Catherine Maughon was 34. No records appear for Patsy after 1900. It isn't clear as to whether she died as a child or there just are not records available to support her later years.

Patsy Maughon and her siblings were living in Pike County, Alabama in 1900 when the boll weevil devastated nearby cotton fields. By 1915, the devastating boll weevil had eaten its way through much of the American South's cotton crop. The "wave of evil" proved to be a costly nuisance for southern farmers. Ineffective government-sponsored measures drove locals to turn to folk remedies in hopes of protecting their lucrative crop. While some sprayed their fields with ash, others drowned the swarming beetles in kerosene. With females laying 200 eggs every 10 days, these insect-fighting attempts failed miserably. Between 1914 and 1917, cotton production was down 70 percent in Alabama alone. Southern agriculture took a huge hit and its labor force, mostly African American sharecroppers, found themselves out of work. Tens of thousands headed North in a mass exodus named the Great Migration. By the 1920s, though the beetles had almost disappeared, their infestation had lasting effects on southern agriculture. Farmers began diversifying their crops to include other staples like corn and wheat. The boll weevil monument built in 1919 in nearby Enterprise, Alabama commemorates this positive outcome from the infestation. Farmers such as Pvt. John Angle Maughon suffered thru the devastation but did not let the boll weevil win.

The sixth child born unto Pvt. John Angle Maughon and Emily Catherine Maughon was a daughter named Oatsie Maughon Stinson. When Oatsie Maughon Stinson was born in 1899 in Pike County, Alabama her father, Pvt. John Angle Maughon was 62, and her mother, Emily Catherine Maughon was 37. She married Preston Stinson on March 26, 1924 in Pike County, Alabama. Census records indicate that they had one child during their marriage. No further records were available to verify other children if any. Oatsie Maughon Stinson died on November 14, 1985 in Phenix City, Alabama at the age of 86, and was buried with her husband.

The seventh child of Pvt. John Angle Maughon and Emily Catherine Amos Maughon was a daughter named Leona "Leo" Maughon Galloway. When Leo Maughon Galloway was born on November 25, 1901 in Pike County, Alabama her father, Pvt. John Angle Maughon was 64, and her mother, Emily Catherine Amos Maughon was 39. She married Davis Wheeler Galloway on April 10, 1920 in Pike County, Alabama. Davis Wheeler Galloway spent his life working as a road foreman for the State and help over the building of many of the new roads and bridges in the county. They had seven children in 15 years. Her children includes: Doris Elizabeth Galloway Stewart married to James Roscoe Stewart, Morris D. Galloway married to Mary Dean Nicholson Galloway, Daynor Colbert Galloway, Davis Wilbur Galloway married to Gertrude Daniels Galloway, Patricia Ann Galloway Maddox, Noah Galloway and John Galloway. Leona Maughon Galloway was always lovingly known by all who knew her as "MaMa Leo". Leona "Leo" Maughon Galloway died on May 7, 1984 in Brundidge, Alabama at the age of 82 and was buried in Pike County, Alabama at St. John Baptist Church Cemetery in the Tarentum Community alongside her husband.

The eighth and youngest child of Pvt. John Angle Maughon and Emily Catherine Maughon was a daughter named Ruby Clarice Maughon Stinson. When Ruby Maughon Stinson was born on November 26, 1905 in Pike County, Alabama her father, Pvt. John Angle Maughon was 68 and her mother, Emily Catherine Amos Maughon was 43. She married Homer Stinson on December 6, 1920 in Pike County, Alabama. They had two children during their marriage. She died as a young mother on April 22, 1928 in Orlando, Florida at the age of 22, and was buried in Pike County, Alabama at the St. John Baptist Church Cemetery in the Tarentum Community.

The family of Pvt. John Angle Maughon and Emily Catherine Maughon witnessed many changes through the passages of time including the Civil War, World War I and World War II, the sweltering heatwave of the 1930s, the tumultuous boll weevil havoc of the early 1900s and the Great Depression era. The family is made up of the strong ties that bind and come from hard working honest stock. The family has contributed significantly to the growth and development of Pike County, more specifically to the town of Brundidge, Alabama and to the Tarentum and the Tennille Communities. The surnames of Allen, Amos, Black, Brooks, Caldwell, Dickey, Flowers, Galloway, Griswold, Heard, Jackson, Johnston, Shiver, Stinson, Whittington and Wilson are all well known, respected and loved families that are directly connected to the John Angle Maughon Family.

Wiley Anjel Buchannan Maughon and Sarah Freeman Maughon's eleventh child born unto them was a son named James Robert "Jas" Maughon. When Pvt. James R. "Jas" Maughon was born on August 1, 1840 in Walton County, Georgia his father, Wiley Anjel Buchannan Maughon was 64 and his mother, Sarah Freeman Maughon was 40. He married Mary "Mollie" Taylor Maughon Davis on July 21, 1873 in Pike County, Alabama. They had ten children in 27 years. He died on February 2, 1910 in Pike County, Alabama at the age of 69 and was buried there in the St. John Baptist Church Cemetery alongside his wife. James Robert Maughon made his way to Pike County, Alabama sometime between the close of the Civil War in 1865 and 1880. James Robert Maughon first entered the service to fight for his beloved south during the Civil War as a Private in March 1861 in Monroe, Georgia. He served in the 11th Georgia Regiment Company H and served until the close of war and was paroled at Appomattox, Virginia in April 1865.

James Robert "Jas" Maughon

Mary "Mollie" Taylor Maughon

Mary "Mollie" Taylor Maughon and three of her grandchildren

The 11th Georgia Infantry was organized and mustered into Confederate service in the early spring of 1861. Some of the companies had enlisted before the firing on Fort Sumter. The 11th regiment served in Anderson's Brigade, Field's Division, Longstreet's Corps and Army of Northern Virginia. They served throughout the war in Virginia from First Manassas through Appomattox. They accompanied Longstreet to Tennessee in 1863 and participated in Chickamauga and the siege of Knoxville. The battles that they entailed are as follows: First Manassas, Yorktown, New Bridge, Seven Days, Rappahannock Station, Second Manassas, Sharpsburg, Fredericksburg, Suffolk, Gettysburg, Funks town, Charleston, Chickamauga, Chattanooga, Knoxville, Wilderness, Petersburg and finally at Appomattox by General Robert E. Lee's side upon the surrender to General Ulysses S. Grant on April 9, 1865.

After five long devouring years in service, James Robert Maughon returned home and shortly after moved to Pike County, Alabama with his brothers, Mitchell Dooley Maughon and John Angle Maughon. James Robert Maughon settled down four miles south of Brundidge, Alabama on the McWaters School Road near the Tarentum Community to a life of farming. His farm was one of about two hundred acres that was always under a high rate of cultivation. He married Mary "Mollie Taylor and began his life as a husband, father and hardworking successful farmer. Mary "Mollie" Taylor Maughon was the eighth of ten children born to Ezekial Henry Taylor and Mary Sykes Taylor of the Bethlehem community just west of Brundidge, Alabama. She was the granddaughter of the Honorable Ezekial Taylor and Mary Kellum Taylor also of the Bethlehem community. The Honorable Ezekial Taylor was the area circuit judge in his home of Pulaski County, Georgia. Mary "Mollie" Taylor Maughon's father, Ezekial Henry Taylor was a well-respected man of Brundidge, Alabama and also was known for his service as a Grand Mason. The Brundidge Masonic Lodge # 184 was formed in 1853. Ezekial Henry Taylor was there throughout the initial conception of the lodge. Mary "Mollie" Taylor Maughon's siblings include:

Nancy Winfred Taylor McGowan Youngblood who was first married to Thomas D.S. McGowan who was a sergeant in the 45th Alabama

Infantry Regiment Company E, during the Civil War. Thomas D.S. McGowan was killed during the battle of Murfreesboro in Tennessee. He never returned home and was buried on the grounds of the University of Tennessee Chattanooga Campus on December 1, 1862. After the death of her husband, Nancy married again to John W. Youngblood with whom she had 9 children with in addition to her first three with Thomas D.S. McGowan.

Mary "Mollie" Taylor Maughon's brother, Pvt. Oliver Taylor also died during the battle of Murfreesboro. He was also enlisted in the 45th Alabama Infantry Company R. Pvt. Oliver Taylor is buried at the National Cemetery in Nashville, Tennessee. Mary "Mollie Taylor Maughon's sister, Louisa Elizabeth Taylor Rainer married Joel J. Rainer. The couple settled and raised their family in Crenshaw County, Alabama. Both Louisa and Joel J. Rainer are buried at the Oakwood Cemetery in Troy, Alabama. Mary "Mollie" Taylor Maughon also had a brother named Ezekial Taylor. Records include him in the 1850 census with his parents and siblings but he doesn't appear in any records after that time. Other sources show that he may have died in Texas, but no death year is indicated. Mary "Mollie" Taylor Maughon's brother, Seth Kellum Taylor married his first wife, Alice Victoria Lee Taylor in 1873. Records show that she died in 1880 during childbirth. Seth Kellum Taylor and his first wife Alice Victoria Lee Taylor had four children together, Edward Taylor, Clarence Ezekial Taylor, Joseph Kellum Taylor and Alice V. Taylor born in 1880. Shortly following her death, Seth Kellum Taylor marries her sister, Susan Eugenia Lee Taylor. Together Seth and Susan had five additional children, Elizabeth "Lizzie" Taylor, Needham Howell Taylor, Willie E. Taylor, Walter Lorenzo Taylor, and Grover Palmer Taylor. Seth Kellum Taylor served in the U.S. Navy. After his service in the Navy he was inaugurated into the Slipup Community post office as the postmaster in 1901. Seth Kellum Taylor and his family are lifelong Brundidge, Alabama residents. Seth Kellum Taylor is buried in the Old Brundidge City Cemetery alongside both Alice

Victoria Lee Taylor and Susan Eugenia Lee Taylor. Mary "Mollie" Taylor Maughon's brother, Kesloe or Kelsoe Taylor. The last indication of records for Kesloe/Kelsoe Taylor is the 1870 Pike County Census showing him to be 17 years old and living at home with his parents. Nothing appears for him after that time. Mary "Mollie" Taylor Maughon's brother named Charles "Snap" Taylor. Charles "Snap" Taylor married Sarah Catherine Cook Taylor. They settled in Turnersville, Coryell County, Texas. Charles "Snap" Taylor died in 1932 and is buried at the Turnersville Cemetery in Coryell County, Texas alongside his wife. Mary "Mollie" Taylor Maughon's youngest sibling was a brother named John P. Taylor who was a lifelong Brundidge, Alabama native. John P. Taylor married Edie Helms Taylor. Both John P. and Edie are buried in the Bethlehem Baptist Church Cemetery and are lifelong residents of Brundidge, Alabama.

Within a year, James Robert Maughon and Mary "Mollie" Taylor Maughon's first child was born. The child was a daughter named Sallie Lee Maughon McWaters. When Sallie Lee Maughon McWaters was born in September 1874 in Pike County, Alabama her father, Pvt. James Robert "Jas" Maughon was 34, and her mother, Mary "Mollie" Taylor Maughon was 17. She married William Uriah McWaters in 1891 in Pike, Alabama. William Uriah McWaters was the son of William Pierce McWaters and Nancy Ellen Fuller McWaters of the Victoria Community in Coffee County, Alabama. Sallie Lee Maughon McWaters and William Uriah McWaters had six children in 16 years. Their children include: Anna Lee Ellen McWaters Brooks married to James Britton Brooks, Mattie Temper McWaters Stewart married to Joseph Henry Stewart, James WD McWaters, Burnice Asberry McWaters married to Eathel Strength McWaters, Eddis Karo McWaters married to Ollie Bee Flowers McWaters, and Andrew J. McWaters married to Bessie Corrine Graham McWaters. Sallie Lee Maughon McWaters died on March 25, 1953 in Tarentum, Alabama at the age of 78. William Uriah McWaters died December 27, 1953 in Tarentum, Alabama. They are both buried at St. John Baptist Church Cemetery in Tarentum, Alabama.

L to R: Cora Maughon Flowers, Thomas George Maughon, Sallie Lee Maughon McWaters, and Mary Ella Mae Maughon Simmons Jackson

The second child born unto James Robert "Jas" Maughon and Mary "Mollie Taylor Maughon was daughter named Mary Ella Maughon Simmons Jackson married first to William L. Simmons. William L. Simmons died August 9, 1926 and is buried at St. John Baptist Church Cemetery. After his death, Mary Ella married Elias Amzie Jackson. Mary Ella Maughon Simmons Jackson had no children of her own. She is buried next to her first husband, William L. Simmons, at St. John Baptist Church Cemetery in Tarentum, Alabama.

Mary Ella "Mae" Maughon Simmons Jackson

The third child of James Robert "Jas" Maughon and Mary "Mollie" Taylor Maughon was a daughter named Mattie Maughon Hoomes. When Mattie Maughon Hoomes was born on November 15, 1879 in Pike County, Alabama her father, Pvt.James Robert "Jas" Maughon was 39, and her mother, Mary "Mollie" Taylor Maughon was 22. She married Enoch Emoniel Hoomes in 1899. Enoch Hoomes worked during his life as a farmer to support his family. They had six children in 14 years. Their children include: Mary Matilda Hoomes Hays who married Jesse Grady Hays, Jr., James Arthur Hoomes who married Bernice Cowart Hoomes, Ollie B. Hoomes Brown who married Fred L. Brown, Nettie Pearl Hoomes Courson who married Cecil Ray Courson, Sr., John Clay Hoomes who married Levis V. Patterson Hoomes and Willis A. Manuel "Bill" Hoomes who married Leona Cash Hoomes. Mattie Maughon Hoomes died on September 5, 1961 in Opp, Alabama at the age of 81, and was buried in Coffee County, Alabama at the Rhoades Cemetery alongside her husband.

The fourth child born unto James Robert "Jas" Maughon and Mary "Mollie" Taylor Maughon was a son named James Robert Mitchell Maughon. When James Robert Mitchell Maughon was born in March 1885 in Pike County, Alabama his father, Pvt. James Robert "Jas" Maughon was 44 and his mother, Mary "Mollie" Taylor Maughon was 27. He had three sons and five daughters with Eleanor "Timmie" Irenia Mauldin Maughon. Their children include: Odis Maughon who married Ivey Virgie Henley Maughon, Eula Lee Maughon McGlaun who married Virgil Lee McGlaun, Leosia "Lessie" Maugham Black who married Edward Black, Tupsey Ree Maughon who was never married, Jimmie Maughon who there are no records for after 1930 and no wife or children are indicated for him, Agnes Edith Maughon Harper who married Woodrow Wilson Harper, Freeman Foy Maughon who married Mildred Powell Maughon, and Cola Jane Maughon Harrison Marshall. James Robert Mitchell Maughon and his family settled in and around the Covington County Area. He died on January 8, 1958 in Opp, Alabama at the age of 72, and is buried at the Hickory Grove Cemetery.

The fifth child of James Robert "Jas" Maughon was a son named Thomas George "Tom" Maughon. When Thomas George "Tom" Maughon was born on May 10, 1886 in Pike County, Alabama his father,

Pvt. James Robert "Jas" Maughon, was 45 and his mother, Mary "Mollie" Taylor Maughon was 28. He married Mary Norton Maughon on January 15, 1905 in his hometown. They had six children in 17 years. Their children include: Katie Bell Maughon Sanders who married Jack H. Sanders and lived in Brundidge, Alabama, John Raymond Maughon who married Virgie A. Lancaster Maughon, Millie Maughon who no records are shown for after 1920, Leroy Maughon who was married to Hazel Mae Maughon, William Henry "Shine" Maughon who was married to Myrtle Shirley Lancaster Maughon, and Mary Emma Maughon Stringer who was married to Paul Louis Stringer. Thomas spent his life working as a brick mason to support his family. Thomas George "Tom" Maughon died on June 1, 1976 in Laurel, Mississippi at the age of 90. He was buried in Goodway, Alabama. His wife, Mary Norton Maughon is buried at Shady Grove Baptist Church in Brundidge, Alabama.

Thomas George "Tom" Maughon

The sixth child of James Robert "Jas" Maughon was a daughter named Annie Mae Maughon Allen. When Annie Mae Maughon Allen was born on January 16, 1888 in Pike County, Alabama her father, Pvt. James Robert "Jas" Maughon was 47, and her mother, Mary "Mollie Taylor Maughon was 30. She had two sons and one daughter with Caswell Asberry Allen between 1911 and 1921. Their children include: Dalton Little Allen who married Obera Virginia Cash Allen, Gladys Mae Allen who died at birth, and Davis C. Allen who married Mary Lou Jordan Allen. Caswell worked as a farmer to support his family. Annie Mae Maughon Allen died on September 4, 1961 in Phenix City, Alabama at the age of 73. Annie is buried next to her husband and newborn baby at St. John Baptist Cemetery in Brundidge, Alabama.

Annie Mae Maughon Allen (Far Left)

The seventh child born unto James Robert "Jas" Maughon and Mary "Mollie" Taylor Maughon was a son named Robert L. "Bob" Maughon. When Robert L. "Bob" Maughon was born on March 10, 1891 in Pike County, Alabama his father, Pvt.James Robert "Jas" Maughon was 50 and his mother, Mary "Mollie" Taylor Maughon was 33. Robert L. Maughon served in the Army during World War I. His service destination was Brest, France where he served in the Company "B" 106th Army Engineers. After returning home to Brundidge, Alabama from the service, he worked as a farm laborer until ill health claimed his life. Census records show that he had one foster son with Sara Johnston Maughon. Their foster son, Harold Kevin Childs was married to Minnie Jewel Tillman Childs of Brundidge, Alabama. Harold was the biological son of Henry and Rebecca Johnston Childs (Sarah's sister). Robert L. "Bob" Maughon died on November 19, 1935 in Brundidge, Alabama at the age of 44. He and Sara are buried at St. John Baptist Church in Brundidge, Alabama. Their foster son, Harold Childs and his wife, Jewel Childs are buried there as well.

Photo of the Army portrait of Robert L. "Bob" Maughon that hung in Lonnie Ophelia Maughon Norton's home

The eighth child born unto James Robert "Jas" Maughon and Mary "Mollie" Taylor Maughon was a daughter named Lonnie Ophelia Maughon Norton. When Lonnie Ophelia Maughon Norton was born on August 30, 1893, in Brundidge, Pike County, Alabama her father, Pvt. James Robert "Jas" Maughon was 53 and her mother, Mary "Mollie" Taylor Maughon was 35. She married William Henry Norton on December 11, 1910 in Brundidge, Pike County, Alabama. Their wedding was performed at St. John Baptist Church in Brundidge, Alabama by Calvin A. Whittington. William Henry Norton and Lonnie Ophelia Maughon Norton had seven children in 24 years.

Children of James R. and Mary Taylor Maughon
Standing: Mary Ella Mae Maughon Jackson, Jesse Stattings Maughon
Sitting: Lonnie Ophelia Maughon Norton and Cora Maughon Flowers
Circa 1905

(L) Lonnie Ophelia Maughon Norton and her mother, Mary "Mollie" Taylor Maughon

William Henry Norton and Lonnie Ophelia Maughon Norton
on their wedding day, December 11, 1910 at
St. John Baptist Church in Tarentum, Pike County, Alabama

William Henry Norton and Lonnie Ophelia Maughon Norton on their wedding day, December 11, 1910 at St. John Baptist Church in Tarentum, Pike County, Alabama

Lonnie Ophelia Maughon Norton and her first child, Ella Mae Norton Stewart, circa 1915

Lonnie Ophelia Maughon Norton

Lonnie Ophelia Maughon Norton and Rusty Norton

William Henry Norton and Lonnie Ophelia Maughon Norton
50th wedding Anniversary 1960

(L to R) Bobby Norton (youngest child of
William Henry and Lonnie Norton), William Henry Norton
and John Norton (oldest child of JD Norton and oldest
grandchild of William Henry and Lonnie Norton) circa 1940.

William Henry Norton circa 1960

William Henry Norton and Rusty Norton at the home place on Hwy. 125 in Brundidge, Al.

William Henry Norton

William Henry Norton's father was Henry Durant "Dewey" Norton who migrated to Pike County sometime between 1850 and 1860. 1850 Census records show Henry Durant "Dewey" Norton living in Marlboro County, South Carolina. 1860 census records show him living in Coffee County, Alabama. He later moved and settled in Pike County, Alabama with his wife, Elnore Nancy Clementine "Clemmie" Crenshaw Norton in about 1885. He was a prominent member of the Milo community in the Springhill area of Pike County, Alabama. Henry joined the Masonic lodge in 1901 and served until his death in 1935. Clemmie Crenshaw Norton was born and raised in the Dale County, Alabama community known as Rocky Head. Henry Durant "Dewey" Norton's father was Wesley Norton, also from Marlboro County, South Carolina. Wesley Norton enlisted in the Army where he ranked as Private. His enlistment date was June 1, 1861. He served in the 15th Alabama Infantry, Company D Regiment. Wesley had just prior to the Civil War moved to Pike County, Alabama where he married Orpha "Orpa" Bundy Norton from the Spring Hill community. Wesley died in battle sometime during 1862. He never returned home from the war.

The 15th Alabama Infantry mustered 1,633 men during the Civil War, of whom 260 were killed in action and 440 died of disease. It has become famous as the Confederate regiment that attacked Union Colonel Joshua Lawrence Chamberlain's Twentieth Maine at Little Round Top in the Battle of Gettysburg.

The 15th organized eleven companies at Fort Mitchell, Alabama, under Colonel James Cantey and Major John W.L. Daniel. In August 1861 they were moved by train to Richmond and then ordered to the frontlines of battle. The regiment suffered heavily from a harsh epidemic of measles and by the winter of 1861 over 200 men died from the disease. A hospital was established for the regiment's sick at the St. Paul's Episcopal Church in Haymarket, Virginia. The regimental Surgeon, 75 year old Dr. Francis A. Stanford, put in 18 hour days tending the sick. Captain Oates visited the hospital and commented that "It was no uncommon sight at that hospital to see six or seven corpses of the 15th Alabama regiment's men laid out all at once." The regiment was present during all of the following battles: Battle of Front Royal, Battle of Winchester, Battle of Cross Keys, First Battle of Cold Harbor, Battle of Malvern Hill, Hazel River, Manassas Junction, Second Battle of Manassas, Battle of Chantilly, Siege of Harpers Ferry, Battle of Sharpsburg (Antietam), Boteler's Ford, Battle of Fredericksburg, Suffolk Campaign, Battle of Gettysburg, Battle of Chickamauga, Brown's Ferry and Lookout Valley, Siege of Knoxville, Bean's Station, Battle of the Wilderness, Battle of Spotsylvania Court House, Hanover Court House and Second Battle of Cold Harbor, Deep Bottom, Fussel's Mill and was present at Appomattox Court House where the regiment surrendered it's remaining 17 officers and 170 men under Captain Eli Daniel Clower.

Henry Durant "Dewey" Norton and
Nancy Clementine "Clemmie" Crenshaw Norton, circa 1930.

Henry Durant "Dewey" Norton's siblings include: Elizabeth Norton Lucas who married William Lucas from Elba, Alabama. Elizabeth and William are both buried at Center Ridge Cemetery in Pike County, Alabama. Henry Durant "Dewey Norton's brother, Pvt. William Robert Norton who married Permilia Shiver Norton after the death of his first wife, Selivia Norton in 1869. Pvt. William Robert Norton and Selivia had one son together before her death. Pvt. William Robert and Permilia Shiver Norton had seven children together. Pvt. William Robert Norton enlisted in the 54th Alabama Infantry Company A during the Civil War. He and his wife, Permilia are buried at Christian Home Cemetery in Newton, Alabama.

The 54th Alabama Infantry Regiment was made up of six Alabama companies of the First Alabama-Miss-Tenn. Regiment of Col. Baker of Barbour County, Alabama and four Alabama companies of the regiment of Col. L. M. Walker of Tennessee. These companies had been captured at Island Ten, after nearly a year's arduous service above Memphis. Organized at Jackson, Miss, October 1862, the Fifty-fourth operated in the vicinity of Vicksburg during the winter. It fought at Fort Pemberton with light loss, and at Baker's Creek with equal result. Having escaped Vicksburg by moving with Gen. Loring from Baker's Creek, the Fifty-fourth was soon after at the siege of Jackson. It was then transferred to the army of Gen. Bragg. The regiment wintered at Dalton, and was engaged in the campaign from there to Atlanta, when the Army of Tennessee disputed the ground inch by inch, and stained those inches with blood. The regiment lost severely at Resaca and at Atlanta July 22. The loss was very heavy at Atlanta July 28, more than half the regiment being killed and wounded, and the flag perforated by forty bullets. Having moved with Hood into middle Tennessee, the Fifty-fourth shared the privations and disasters of that campaign. Transferred to North Carolina, its colors waved defiantly at Bentonville, its last battlefield. A remnant only was surrendered with the forces of Gen. Johnston.

Henry Durant "Dewey" Norton's brother, Berry Franklin Norton married Lavinia "Vinie" Lightfoot Norton. Berry and Vinie settled and raised their family in the Center Ridge Community in Pike County, Alabama. Berry worked for many years of his life as a successful farmer in Center

Ridge. Berry Franklin Norton and Lavinia "Vinie" Lightfoot Norton are both buried at the Center Ridge Cemetery in Pike County, Alabama. Henry Durant "Dewey" Norton's sister, Isabel Norton Johnson married Isaac Jefferson Johnson. They settled in the Zion Chapel Community in Coffee County, Alabama. They are both buried at Bluff Springs Cemetery in Coffee County, Alabama.

Henry Durant "Dewey" Norton's sister, Axia Ann Norton was born in 1850 and lived less than a year, she died in 1851 and is buried in Marlboro, South Carolina.

Henry Durant "Dewey" Norton's sister, Mary Jane Norton Rowland married William R. Rowland. They settled and raised their family in Samson, Geneva County, Alabama. They are both buried at the Corner Creek Upper Cemetery located in Hacoda, Geneva County, Alabama.

Henry Durant "Dewey" Norton's brother, Silas Jacob Norton was born in 1854. Silas Jacob Norton doesn't show up in any census records after the 1860 census. He was listed as six years old in 1860. Henry Durant "Dewey" Norton's sister, Sarah Norton Rowell married James C. Rowell. They are listed as living in Coffee County, Alabama. No other records indicate where they are buried.

The youngest sibling of Henry Durant "Dewey" Norton was a sister named Missouri Grenada Green. Missouri Norton married Sanford Z. Green and settled to raise their children in Elba, Coffee County, Alabama. Both Missouri and Sanford are buried at Woodlawn Grove Baptist Church located in Coffee County, Alabama.

Lonnie Ophelia Maughon Norton and William Henry Norton's children include their first born son, J.D. Norton born November 11, 1911 in Brundidge, Alabama. Between 1935 and 1940, J.D. moved from Brundidge, Alabama to Columbus, Georgia where he began working in the Swift Spinning Mill. There he registered for the Army Draft of World War II. On November 9, 1933, he married Myra Gladys Brooks of Brundidge, Alabama. Myra Gladys Brooks Norton's parents were

John Marshall Brooks and Elizabeth Lavinia "Lizzie" Lewis Brooks of the Tarentum Community in Pike County, Alabama. In 1935, J.D and Gladys' first son was born, John William Norton who married Lorene Hudson Norton. In 1938 their second son was born, Jerry Buford Norton who married Carolyn Waltman Norton. In 1940 their third son was born, James Gary Norton who married Annie Louise Reeves Norton. J.D. and Gladys Norton's family all settled in and around the Columbus, Georgia and Phenix City, Alabama area. J. D. Norton died on November 28, 1972, in Phenix City, Alabama, at the age of 61. He is buried at the LaDonia Baptist Church Cemetery in Phenix City, Alabama. Myra Gladys Brooks Norton died on December 29, 1999 at the age of 89. She is buried next to her husband, JD Norton at the LaDonia Baptist Church Cemetery.

JD Norton

JD Norton and Gladys Brooks Norton

JD and Gladys Brooks Norton with their children, John William Norton, Jerry Buford Norton and James Gary Norton

William Henry Norton and Lonnie Ophelia Maughon Norton's second child was a daughter named Ella Mae Norton Stewart. Ella Mae Norton Stewart was born on November 18, 1913 in Brundidge, Alabama. On May 30, 1931 at the age of 17, she married Floyd Clayton Stewart age 22, of New Brockton, Coffee County, Alabama. After their marriage, Ella Mae and Floyd moved to Santa Rosa, Florida where they started their family and their life together. Floyd Clayton worked as a successful farmer to support his family. He became a well-respected father, husband and member of the Santa Rosa community. Ella Mae Norton Stewart and Floyd Clayton Stewart had 7 children in 13 years.

Ella Mae Norton Stewart and Floyd Clayton Stewart's children include their first born daughter, Loni Murl Stewart Diamond who married Albert Colin Diamond. They had three children: Linda Gail Diamond Baxley who married Kenneth Stewart Baxley, Glenda Diane Diamond Griswold who married Martin Dewayne Griswold and Donna Diamond. Census records do not include any marriage information for Donna Diamond. The children of Ella Mae and Floyd Clayton Stewart all reside in and around the Jay, Santa Rosa, Florida area. Floyd Clayton Stewart died at the age of 66 on November 7, 1974 and Ella Mae Norton Stewart died on March 21, 1977 at the age of 63. They are both buried side by side at the Cora Baptist Church Cemetery in Jay, Santa Rosa, Florida.

Ella Mae Norton Stewart and Floyd Clayton Stewart's second child was a daughter named Reba Nell Stewart Barlow. Reba Nell Stewart Barlow married John David Barlow, Sr. in 1955. John David Barlow, Sr. served in the US Navy during his lifetime. Census information that is available lists no children for them. Reba Nell Stewart Barlow died on July 2, 2000 and is buried at Cora Baptist Church in Jay, Santa Rosa, Florida. John David Barlow, Sr. died on December 11, 2005 and is buried next to his wife.

Ella Mae Norton Stewart and Floyd Clayton Stewart's third child was a son named Clayton Junior Stewart. Clayton Junior was married to Pearlie Louise Barlow Stewart. Pearlie and Clayton Junior married in Pike County, Alabama in 1955. They later moved to Santa Rosa, Florida where they had four children in 10 years. Their children include: Ann Elizabeth Stewart Polk who married Eddie Wayne Polk, Michael Clayton

Stewart who married Deanna Kay Odom Stewart, Stephanie Stewart and Brenda Stewart Pearson who married Larry Eugene Pearson. The family of Clayton Junior and Pearlie Louise Stewart all settled in and around the Santa Rosa, Florida area. Clayton Junior Stewart died on August 12, 2017 in Santa Rosa, Florida at the age of 81 and was buried in Jay, Santa Rosa, Florida at the Cora Baptist Church Cemetery. Pearlie Louise Barlow Stewart died on April 12, 2011 in Jay, Santa Rosa, Florida at the age of 82, and was buried there at the Cora Baptist Church Cemetery alongside her husband.

Ella Mae Norton Stewart and Floyd Clayton Stewart's fourth child was a daughter named Myra Sue Stewart Griffith. Myra Sue Stewart Griffith was born on May 21, 1938 in Pike County, Alabama her father, Floyd Clayton Stewart was 29 and her mother, Ella Mae Norton Stewart was 24. She married James Barney "JB" Griffith in June 1956 in Santa Rosa County, Florida. JB Griffith was a native of Pace, Florida and a U.S. Army Veteran. He was also a retired truck driver. They had three children during their marriage. Their children include: Amanda Sue Griffith Greene who married Wesley Greene, Sandra Dee Griffith Bush who married Devin Bush of Elba, Alabama, and James Stewart Griffith who married Genevieve Terese Hudson Griffith. Ella Mae Norton Stewart died on May 3, 1999 in Pensacola, Florida at the age of 60. James Barney "JB" Griffith died October 26, 2015 and is buried next to his wife at the Serenity Gardens Cemetery in Santa Rosa County, Florida.

Ella Mae Norton Stewart and Floyd Clayton Stewart's fifth child was a son, Jimmie Stewart who died at birth on December 30, 1944.

Ella Mae Norton Stewart and Floyd Clayton Stewart's sixth child was a son named Floyd Clyde Stewart, Sr. Floyd Clyde Stewart, Sr. was born on January 30, 1946 in Jay, Florida. His father, Floyd was 37 and his mother, Ella was 32. He married Brenda Maurine Geiger Stewart in July 1969 in Santa Rosa, Florida. Floyd Clyde Stewart, Sr. was a lifelong resident of Jay, Florida. He was a member of New Bethel Baptist Church in Jay, Florida. He was also a foreman at Moore Creek Mt. Carmel Waterworks. Floyd Clyde Stewart, Sr. and Brenda Stewart had three children during their marriage. Their children include: Clyde "Pee Wee" Stewart, Chad Stewart and Casey Stewart married to Michelle Stewart. Floyd Clyde

Stewart, Sr. died on May 10, 1999, in his hometown at the age of 53.

Ella Mae Norton and Floyd Clayton Stewart's seventh child was a son named Paul Norton Stewart. Paul Norton Stewart was born on January 7, 1949 in Jay, Florida. He married Joyce Earline Burch Stewart on April 30, 1971 in Escambia County, Florida. The available census records do not indicate the names of any children they may have.

Ella Mae Norton Stewart, circa 1915

Ella Mae Norton Stewart and Floyd Clayton Stewart

Ella Mae Norton Stewart and her family likely experienced an influx of military personnel and tourists during World War II while living in Santa Rosa, Florida. Florida was a hive of activity during World War II. The warm climate and vast amounts of vacant coastal land made it a perfect place to build military bases and train soldiers. New bases were built and old naval stations were reactivated. The training facilities became so crowded, the military took over hundreds of hotels—such as the Don CeSar on St. Pete Beach and the Biltmore Hotel in Miami—for military personnel. Because of its location, Florida was also vital to the United States' defense operations, including the Gulf Sea Frontier, the Eastern Defense Command, and the Civil Air Patrol. German submarines, known as U-boats, were a threat and sank 24 ships off the Florida coast during the war. War contracts in Florida boosted the economy significantly, a welcome side effect in the years after the Depression. The population in Florida boomed during this time too, particularly in Key West and Miami.

Harry S. Truman became president of the shocked and grief-stricken United States upon the death of Franklin D. Roosevelt in 1945. On April 12, 1945, the United States was dealt a terrible blow with the unexpected death of President Franklin D. Roosevelt. Beloved by his country, President Roosevelt had led Americans through both the Great Depression and a World War. Responsibilities regarding the ongoing war now fell on the shoulders of Harry S. Truman. Only two hours after hearing of the death of President Roosevelt, Truman received the presidential oath of office from Chief Justice Harlan F. Stone in the Cabinet Room of the White House, becoming the 33rd U.S. President. Many difficult decisions instantly became his, including whether to drop atomic bombs on Japan. "I felt like the moon, the stars, and all the planets had fallen on me," he later told reporters. President Truman asked the cabinet of Franklin D. Roosevelt to stay on with him and was later re-elected. These major events in our country's history were experienced by Ella Mae Norton Stewart and her family firsthand.

Lonnie Ophelia Norton Maughon and William Henry Norton's third child was a son named Luico Norton. When Luico Norton was born on April 20, 1915 in Pike County, Alabama his father, William Henry Norton was 27 and his mother, Lonnie Ophelia Maughon Norton was 21. He married Jewell Mae Petty Norton and they had three children together.

Luico Norton and Jewel Mae Petty's first born child was a son named Louie Shelby Norton. When Louie Shelby Norton was born on October 3, 1937 in Columbus, Georgia his father, Luico Norton, was 22 and his mother, Jewell Mae Petty Norton was 16. He married Betty Sue West Norton Lethco on April 17, 1957 in Winston-Salem, North Carolina. They had one child during their marriage. Louie Shelby Norton served in the U.S. Navy in Korea from 1955 thru 1957. He died on August 8, 2002 in Phenix City, Alabama at the age of 64, and was buried in The Ft. Mitchell National Cemetery in Ft. Mitchell, Alabama.

Louico Norton and Jewell Mae Petty Norton's second child was a daughter named Mary Nell Norton McFarland. When Mary Nell Norton McFarland was born in 1939 in Columbus, Georgia her father, Luico, was 24, and her mother, Jewell was 19. No other census data was available for Mary Nell Norton indicating her spouse's name or any children.

Luico Norton and Jewell Mae Petty Norton's third child was a son named Larry Ronald Norton, Sr. When Larry Ronald Norton, Sr. was born on December 21, 1942 in Columbus, Georgia his father, Luico Norton was 27 and his mother, Jewell Mae Petty Norton was 22. He had four sons and three daughters with Kathy Norton. He died on August 10, 2011 at the age of 68 and was buried in Phenix City, Alabama at the Lakeview Memory Gardens Cemetery.

Luico Norton also had three daughters with Xray Peak Arnett Norton. Their three daughters include a daughter named Jimmie Faye Norton Maulden, a daughter named Winnie Jewell Norton Hunter, and a daughter named Dottie Norton Steely. Luico Norton also had one son and one daughter with Mary Claud Arnett Norton. Their children include a son named Franky Norton and a daughter named Cathy Norton Sport. During his lifetime, Luico worked as a very young man in the Swift Spinning Mill in Columbus, Georgia with his brothers. Later on, he joined the U.S. Army where he served as a Private during World War II. During the war he received a Bronze Star Medal as well as the Purple Heart. He lived for the most part of his life in Luverne, Alabama with his loving wife, Mary Claud Norton of 53 years. He died on October 29, 2009 in Luverne, Alabama at the age of 94. Luico Norton was buried at the Emmaus Cemetery in Luverne, Crenshaw County, Alabama.

Pvt. Luico Norton
US Army, World War II
Circa 1942

Lonnie Ophelia Maughon Norton and William Henry Norton's fourth child was a son named Harvey Buford Norton, Sr. Harvey Buford Norton was born on March 11, 1917 in Pike County, Alabama his father, William Henry Norton was 29 and his mother, Lonnie Ophelia Maughon Norton was 23. He married Ellen Beatrice Hawke Norton on December 18, 1943. Harvey served in the U.S. Army during World War II. His enlistment dates were November 18, 1942 thru November 2, 1945. After serving in the Army, Harvey made his home in Leary, Georgia where he lived for 44 years. He was a well-respected and loved member of the Leary Community. He served as deacon emeritus at Leary Baptist Church. Harvey worked for many years to support his family at the Jordan farms, now known as McLendon-Webb Farm, Inc. They had three children in 10 years. Their children include: Harvey Buford Norton, Jr. who married Marilyn Sawyer Norton, Josephine Norton Stripling who married Charles Lamar Stripling, Sr., and Bobby Ray Norton who married Astrid Norton. Harvey Buford Norton, Jr. died on May 8, 1993 in Leary, Georgia, at the age of 76. Ellen Beatrice Hawke Norton died on November 7, 1997 in Leary, Calhoun County, Georgia.

**Pvt. Harvey Buford Norton
U. S. Army during World War II 1942**

L to R: Frazier Norton, Harvey Buford Norton and best friend, Lamar Lewis circa, 1942 Photo taken on the old Pea River Bridge on Hwy. 231 south of Brundidge, AL.

L to R: Harvey Buford Norton, Lamar Lewis, Frazier Norton, and Leon Leatherwood, Circa 1942

L to R: Harvey Buford Norton, Lonnie Ophelia Maughon Norton and Frazier Norton

Frazier Norton and Beatrice Hawke Norton, wife of Harvey Norton

Lonnie Ophelia Maughon Norton and William Henry Norton's fifth child was a son named Frazier Norton. When Frazier Norton was born on April 24, 1919 in Pike County, Alabama his father, William Henry Norton was 31 and his mother, Lonnie Ophelia Maughon Norton, was 25. As a young man, he first worked at the Swift Spinning Mill in Columbus, Georgia. He entered the U.S. Army on September 29, 1942 and served in World War II. His service included a Medical Detachment where he worked as a hospital orderly. He received an honorable discharge on April 1, 1944. Prior to leaving the Army he worked as an airplane mechanic in Sylmar, California. After returning home to Brundidge, Alabama he began working as a mechanic in a local shop in the Tarentum Community and later on began working as a diesel mechanic for the Leaseway truck lines which was contracted thru the Doxie Foods Corporation in Brundidge, Alabama, here he worked until he retired in the early 1980's. Frazier Norton had one son named Ronald Norton with Mary Jewel Renfroe Norton to whom he was first married to in 1941. Ronald Norton married Mary Irene Hodge Norton. Ronald and Irene have one daughter, Amy Norton Minor of Pike County, Alabama. Frazier Norton later married Hazel Alene Byrd Norton on July 16, 1947 in Dale County, Alabama. They had seven children together.

Frazier Norton and Hazel Alene Byrd Norton's children include their firstborn, Linda Jeanette Norton McKim who married Captain Glenn C. McKim. When Linda Jeanette Norton McKim was born on October 25, 1949 in Pike County, Alabama her father, Frazier Norton was 30 and her mother, Hazel Alene Byrd Norton was 18. She had two daughters with Capt. Glenn Cameron McKim between 1972 and 1975. She died on December 2, 2004, in Enterprise, Alabama, at the age of 55. Linda Jeanette Norton McKim is buried at St. John Baptist Church in the Tarentum community. Linda Jeanette Norton McKim joined the U.S. Air Force soon after graduating from Pike County High School. While in the U. S. Air Force, she served as a Flight nurse during the Vietnam era. While in the U.S. Air Force she met and married her husband, Captain Glenn C. McKim who was a pilot in the U.S. Air Force. Captain Glenn Cameron McKim worked as a pilot until he retired. Linda Jeanette Norton McKim and Captain Glenn C. McKim's two daughters are Karyn Elizabeth McKim

From Walton County, Georgia To Pike County, Alabama

and Kristen Leigh McKim. Linda Jeanette Norton McKim and her husband Captain Glenn C. McKim has had the opportunity to live in many different places which include: Spain, Florida, Georgia, Mississippi, Wyoming, Illinois and Alabama.

Frazier Norton and Hazel Alene Byrd Norton's second born child was a son named John David Norton. When John David Norton was born on January 7, 1951 in Pike County, Alabama his father, Frazier was 31 and his mother, Hazel was 19. John David Norton first married Rachael Parker Norton and together they have one son. John David Norton and Rachael Parker Norton's son is named John David Norton II. John David Norton later married Debbie Holmes Norton. Their children are Tara Thompkins Norris and Houston Taylor Norton. John David Norton worked as a diesel mechanic and truck driver for more than 40 years. He worked for Hudson Industries in Pike County, Alabama and then later for Wiley Sanders Truck Lines in Troy, Alabama. John David Norton has continued to live and remain a native of Pike County, Alabama.

Frazier Norton and Hazel Alene Byrd Norton's third child was a son named Jack Norton. When Jack Norton was born on February 12, 1952 in Dale County, Alabama his father, Frazier was 32 and his mother, Hazel Alene Byrd Norton was 20. He had one son and one daughter with Barbara Ann Maulden Norton. He died on March 15, 1997 in Brundidge, Alabama at the age of 45. He was buried at Shady Grove Baptist Church in Brundidge, Alabama. Jack Norton worked with Wilco Truck lines after graduating from Pike County High School and then later as a truck dispatcher for Hudson Industries in Troy, Alabama. Their children include: Alison Norton Neclerio and Joey Norton. Jack Norton and his wife Barbara Ann Maulden Norton are natives of Brundidge, Pike County, Alabama.

The fourth child of Frazier Norton and Hazel Alene Norton was a daughter named Joann Norton Ziglar Ropp. When Joann Norton Ziglar Ropp was born on August 11, 1953 in Pike County, Alabama her father, Frazier was 34 and her mother, Hazel was 21. Joann Norton married Marion Ziglar and together they have one daughter, Jennifer Marie Ziglar. Joann Norton Ziglar later married Ronald G. Ropp. Joann Norton Ropp worked for many years as a seamstress and has spent many hours caring for her daughter, Jennifer and her husband Ronald Ropp. Ronald Ropp was a veteran of the U.S. Navy and served during the Vietnam Era. Joann Norton Ropp has been a native of both Pike County, Alabama and Coffee County, Alabama. Her husband Ronald Ropp was a native of Missouri; he spent the last years of his life as a native of Coffee County, Alabama.

Frazier Norton and Hazel Alene Byrd Norton's fifth child was a daughter named Debra Jean Norton Berry who married Donnie Len Berry. When Debra Jean Norton Berry was born on May 6, 1955 in Brundidge, Alabama her father, Frazier Norton was 36 and her mother, Hazel Alene Byrd Norton was 23. She married Donnie Len Berry on June 11, 1971. They had two children during their marriage. Their children include: Deborah Lynn Berry Sutton and Richard LaDon Berry of Brundidge, Alabama. Debra Jean Norton Berry spent many years of her life as a seamstress and later worked in a local department store. Donnie Len Berry worked for many years as an insurance sales agent. Debra Jean Norton Berry and her husband Donnie Len Berry are lifelong residents of Brundidge, Pike County, Alabama.

The sixth child born unto Frazier Norton and Hazel Alene Byrd Norton was a son named Dewey LaDon Norton. When Dewey LaDon Norton was born on December 1, 1959 in Pike County, Alabama his father, Frazier Norton was 40 and his mother, Hazel Alene Norton Byrd was 28. Dewey LaDon Norton has worked for many years as a farm caretaker and long haul truck driver. Dewey LaDon Norton has no children of his own but has always loved his nieces and nephews as if they were his own children. Dewey LaDon Norton has spent his life as a resident of Brundidge, Pike County, Alabama and Coffee County, Alabama.

The seventh child born unto Frazier Norton and Hazel Alene Byrd Norton was a daughter named Cynthia Jane Norton Sutton. When Cynthia Jayne Norton Sutton was born on December 10, 1967 in Brundidge, Alabama her father, Frazier Norton was 48 and her mother, Hazel Alene Byrd Norton was 36. She married Gary O'Neal Sutton on December 21, 1990 and they had one daughter together named Garah Candace Sutton. She also had one son with Mark Wallace. Their son is named Cody Montana Wallace. She died on July 8, 2009 in her hometown at the age of 41. Cynthia Jayne Norton Sutton was a lifelong resident of Brundidge, Pike County, Alabama and Coffee County, Alabama.

Frazier Norton enjoyed working in his garden and most of all spending time with his family. He never missed his grandchildren's birthday. He was well known for miles around for his talent as a Ford mechanic. Frazier Norton was also a member of the Brundidge Masonic Lodge # 184 as well as a sixty year member of the local American Legion. He was a member of St. John Baptist Church in Brundidge, Pike County, Alabama. Frazier Norton died on May 19, 1999 in Brundidge, Pike County, Alabama, at the age of 80. He and his wife, Hazel Byrd Norton who died on November 21, 2010 are buried at St. John Baptist Church Cemetery in Brundidge, Alabama.

Frazier Norton

Hazel Alene Byrd Norton

Frazier Norton, Hazel Byrd Norton and their first born, Linda Jeanette Norton McKim, circa 1949

L to R: Floyd Clayton Stewart, Hazel Byrd Norton, Beatrice Hawke Norton, Xray Peak Arnett Norton and Mary Claud Arnett Norton, Circa 1947

**Frazier Norton and first wife, Jewel Renfroe Norton
Circa 1945**

Frazier Norton, Circa 1947

Frazier Norton, circa 1947

Frazier Norton, Circa 1947

Pvt. Frazier Norton during his service in World War II, circa 1942

Pvt. Frazier Norton during his service in World War II, circa 1942

Pvt. Frazier Norton during his service in World War II, circa 1942

Frazier Norton with the Army transport airplane "The Viking" during World War II

Pvt. Frazier Norton and an Army transport airplane during World War II

Frazier Norton and Army plane during World War II

Frazier Norton, Circa 1947

Americans serving in the United States Army were dedicated to ending the Axis assault against freedom during World War II. Frazier Norton and his brothers served in the United States Army during World War II. When the European war came to the United States in 1941, over 8 million American men and women from across the nation answered the call and served in the Army in various capacities, including in segregated units. While many served stateside, such as members of the Women's Army Corps (WACS), Army service took millions to every theater of the war, from Europe and North Africa to the Pacific Islands. About 73 percent of the Army infantry served overseas, for 16 months on average. Most infantrymen coped with poor equipment; went without food, sleep, and shelter; suffered arduous and violent conditions; lived under constant threat of death; and confronted unimaginable horrors. The Army's casualty rate was high: 318,274 were killed and 565,861 injured-- many seriously. Though they often became battle-hardened to survive, in 1943 one soldier wrote, "Don't let anyone tell you that soldiers don't get frightened. They do."

William Henry Norton and Lonnie Ophelia Maughon Norton's sixth child was a son named James Othel Norton. When James Othel Norton was born on November 17, 1921 in Pike County, Alabama his father, William Henry Norton was 33 and his mother, Lonnie Ophelia Maughon Norton was 28. He married Mary Senn Norton on June 14, 1941. They had two children during their marriage. Their first child was a daughter named Janice Mary Norton Burrell who married Rev. Adrian A. Burrell. Their second child was a son named James Murray Norton. James Murray Norton is married to Betty Ann Norton. James Othel Norton served in the U.S. Army as a Staff Sergeant during World War II. He was later employed with Sullivan Lumber Company in Preston, Georgia. James Othel Norton lived in Webster County, Georgia for 58 years and was a member of the Preston Baptist Church. As a hobby, James Othel Norton learned how to make knives and love to work with wood and make windmills. James Othel Norton died at the age of 93 on December 9, 2014 and is buried at the Preston City Cemetery in Preston, Georgia.

Pvt. James Othel Norton during his service in World War II, circa 1942

Mary Senn Norton, Janice Norton and James Othel Norton, Circa 1947

Mary Senn Norton, Murray Norton, Janice Norton and James Othel Norton, Circa 1956

William Henry Norton and Lonnie Ophelia Maughon Norton's seventh child was a son named Bobby Hickman Norton. When Bobby Hickman Norton was born on November 26, 1935 in Pike County, Alabama his father, William Henry Norton was 47 and his mother, Lonnie Ophelia Maughon Norton was 42. He married Lou Merle Wambles Norton on January 31, 1958. They had two children during their marriage. Their two children are Harvey Russell Norton who is married to LaDania Lynn Enfinger Norton and a daughter named Lisa Kaye Norton who died at the age of 5. Bobby Hickman Norton was employed with Fieldcrest Mills with 47 years of loyal service and was retired. He enjoyed all types of automobiles and NASCAR collectables. He loved the outdoors and spending quality time with all his family and especially his grandchildren and great grandchildren. He was a member of Woodland Baptist Church in Ladonia. Bobby Hickman Norton died on August 17, 2018 in Columbus, Georgia at the age of 82. He is buried next to his daughter at the Lakeview Memory Gardens Cemetery in Phenix City, Alabama.

Bobby Hickman Norton, Circa 1936

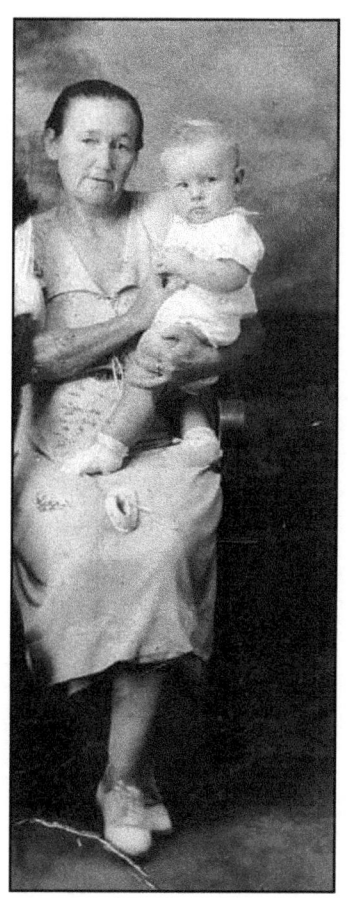

**Lonnie Ophelia Maughon Norton
and Bobby Hickman Norton,
Circa 1936**

William Henry Norton and Bobby Hickman Norton,
Circa 1936

Bobby Hickman Norton, U.S Army 1957

Bobby Hickman Norton and Lou Merle Wambles Norton

Clayton Stewart, Bobby Norton and Lonnie Ophelia Norton

Standing L to R: Frazier Norton, Harvey Norton, Ella Mae Norton Stewart, Luico Norton, And Kneeling L to R: Othel Norton, Bobby Norton and JD Norton, circa 1947

L to R: Bobby Hickman Norton, Frazier Norton,
Beatrice Hawke Norton, Harvey Buford Norton,
Mary Senn Norton and James Othel Norton
1992 Harvey's 75th Birthday Party

L to R: Harvey Buford Norton, James Othel Norton, Bobby Hickman Norton and Frazier Norton, Circa 1992

From Walton County, Georgia To Pike County, Alabama

James Robert "Jas" Maughon and Mary "Mollie Taylor Maughon's ninth child was a son named Jesse Stattings Maughon. When Jesse Stattings Maughon was born on November 10, 1897 in Pike County, Alabama his father, Pvt. James Robert "Jas" Maughon was 57 and his mother, Mary "Mollie" Taylor Maughon was 40. He had four sons and three daughters with Rosa Bell Mobley Maughon between 1916 and 1927. Jesse Stattings Maughon worked for many years until he retired at the Atmore State Prison Farm in Atmore, Alabama as a prison officer. Jesse Stattings Maughon and Rosa Bell Mobley Maughon's children include: a son named James Hubert Maughon who died with his first year of life between 1916 and 1917, he is buried at Union Springs Primitive Baptist Church Cemetery in Brundidge, Alabama, their second child was a son named Robert Edward Maughon, Sr. who was first married to Gladys Elizabeth Jinright Maughon and then to Odie Maughon, their third child was a daughter named Elna Loreane Maughon Houston Hagewood, she was first married to John William Houston and then to Malcolm Hagewood. Jesse Stattings and Rosa Bell's fourth child was a daughter named Grace L. Maughon McCoy who married Claud H. McCoy, they are both buried at St. John Baptist Church Cemetery in Brundidge, Alabama. Jesse Stattings and Rosa Bell's fifth child was a daughter named Evelyn Maughon Parker Sellers, she was first married to Roy H. Parker and then to Arthur M. Sellers, Jr. Jesse Stattings and Rosa Bell's sixth child was a son named George Malcolm Maughon who was married to Ada Mae Taylor Manning Maughon. Their seventh and final child was a son named Jessie Maughon, Jr.; he was married to Sarah Inez Sanders Maughon Mobley. Jesse Stattings Maughon died on November 23, 1956 at the age of 59. He is buried at St. John Baptist Church Cemetery in Brundidge, Alabama. Rosa Bell Mobley Maughon died on December 5, 1979 and she is buried alongside her husband at St. John Baptist Church in Brundidge, Alabama.

Pvt. James Robert "Jas" Maughon and Mary "Mollie" Taylor Maughon's tenth and final child was a daughter named Cora Murphy Maughon Flowers. When Cora Murphy Maughon Flowers was born on March 20, 1901 in Pike County, Alabama her father, Pvt. James Robert "Jas" Maughon, was 60 and her mother, Mary "Mollie" Taylor Maughon was 43. She married James Robert "Rob" Flowers in October 1916 in her hometown. They had three children in 10 years. Their children include: Mary Thelma Flowers Shiver who married Cecil F. Shiver of the Tennille Community in Pike County, Alabama. Mary Thelma and Cecil are buried at the Hamilton Cross Roads Church of Christ Cemetery in Brundidge, Alabama. Their second child was a daughter named Lois Flowers who married Ivan Woodrow Flowers. Lois and Ivan are buried at Williams Chapel United Methodist Church in Brundidge, Alabama. Their third child was a son named Garmon Kenneth Flowers. Garmon Kenneth Flowers married Frances Flowers and was a veteran of the U.S. Air Force from 1951 to 1978. He served during the Korean Conflict. James Robert "Rob" Flowers was the son of Abel and Mary Ellen "Mollie" Dismukes Flowers. He was the grandson of Wingate and Malatha Pate Flowers and great grandson of Luke and Dolly Flowers who were very early settlers of Pike County prior to 1840. All were residents of Brundidge, Alabama and members of the Union Springs Primitive Baptist Church. James Robert "Rob" Flowers served as the church clerk for more than fifty years and also as deacon. He farmed the family farm for more than fifty years located on the McWaters School Road in the Tarentum Community below Brundidge, Alabama. When he died at the age of 91 in 1989, he was the fourth generation and the last surviving church member to be buried at the Union Springs Primitive Baptist Church Cemetery. She died on June 6, 1967 in Pike County, Alabama at the age of 66. Cora Murphy Maughon Flowers is buried next to her husband.

 Wiley Anjel Buchannan Maughon and Sarah Freeman Maughon's youngest child was a son named Thomas George Maughon. When Thomas George Maughon was born on December 1, 1843 in Walton County, Georgia his father, Wiley Anjel Buchannan Maughon was 67 and his mother, Sarah Freeman Maughon was 43. He was never married. He remained in Walton County, Georgia instead of joining his brothers in Pike County, Alabama. He led a very full and rich life, first as a school teacher and later in life he served as Justice of the Peace in Monroe, Georgia. The last eight years of his life he served as the Treasurer of Walton County, Georgia from 1901 until his death in 1908. He died on November 26, 1908 in Monroe, Georgia at the age of 64, and was buried there in the Rest Haven Cemetery.

Children of James R. and Mary Taylor Maughon
L to R:
Cora Murphy Maughon Flowers, Jesse Stattings Maughon,
Lonnie Ophelia Maughon Norton, Mattie Maughon Hoomes,
Thomas George Maughon, James Robert Mitchell Maughon,
Mary Ella Mae Maughon Jackson, Circa 1955

Source Information

Ancestry® | Genealogy, Family Trees & Family History Records, www.ancestry.com/.

"Guides to National Archives Microfilm Publications: Civil War Compiled Service Records." National Archives and Records Administration, National Archives and Records Administration, www.archives.gov/research/alic/reference/military/civil-war-service-records-pamphlets.html.

Royde-Smith, John Graham, and Thomas A. Hughes. "World War II." Encyclopaedia Britannica, Inc., 7 Nov. 2019, www.britannica.com/event/World War II.

I WOULD LIKE to take this opportunity to sincerely thank each of the following family members and friends for the contributions to this work. The pictures and familial information will be forever in print due to your wonderful help and insight on this project. Our ancestors would be so proud of us!

--The family of JD Norton.

--The family of Ella Mae Norton Stewart.

--The family of Luico Norton.

--The family of Harvey Norton,

--The family of Frazier Norton (my grandfather).

--The family of Othel Norton.

--The family of Bobby Norton.

--The family of Estin Black Flowers.

--The family of Leona "Leo" Maughon Galloway.

Lightning Source UK Ltd.
Milton Keynes UK
UKHW011439170620
365157UK00007B/1160